The Crazy Jig

The Crazy Jig

AN ANTHOLOGY OF LESBIAN & GAY WRITING FROM SCOTLAND

Edited by Joanne Winning

With an Introduction
by Iona McGregor

Polygon
EDINBURGH

First published in 1992 by Polygon, 22 George Square, Edinburgh

Individual Contributions © 1992 The Contributors
Preface and selection © 1992 Joanne Winning

Typeset by Combined Arts, Edinburgh
Printed and bound by Billing & Son Ltd,
    Worcester

British Library Cataloguing In Publication Data

The crazy jig
    1. English literature, Scottish writers, 1945-
    Anthologies
    I. Winning, Joanne
    820.8'09411

ISBN 0 7486 6130 1

Set in Monotype Sabon 10.5 on 13.5pt

'Tram-Ride, 1939' by Edwin Morgan is reproduced here by
kind permission of the Mariscat Press.

This book is dedicated to Nessa — without you nothing would be possible.

Contents

Contents

Preface

JOANNE WINNING

CLAMOROUS VOICES indeed. If Carol Rutter hadn't so thoughtlessly used so excellent a title for her book on Shakespearean actresses, I would very much have liked to use it for this book! Our voices as lesbians and gay men are our most important assets, we must never underestimate the noise they can make or the strength with which they empower us. *The Crazy Jig* signifies the continuing commitment of Polygon to publish the voices of lesbian and gay writers in Scotland. Its predecessor *And Thus Will I Freely Sing* and the present volume are the first of their kind in Scotland. But with such clear and strong voices, surely it is time for us to find our place in Scottish publishing and create a platform which gives a larger national and sexual identity. It is simply not enough that there are only two anthologies of our writing in Scotland, because we have a great deal more to say which will benefit both ourselves and the straight community.

Whilst our voices are clear and strong, they are also diverse. I am glad to have edited a collection which in acknowledging a black voice in Scottish Lesbian and Gay writing also acknowledges that presence within our community. Although I'm aware that this presence within the book is not large enough, let us hope that it is the start of something big. The selection balances a man's voice with a woman's voice and the space created for lesbians lets their identity resound through the pages.

There are numerous people whose help and encouragement I must acknowledge. Firstly, Kenny MacLeod since this project was originally intended to be a joint venture. Without Kenny's contacts and faith in me I would not have had the opportunity to edit this book. I would like to thank both Marion and Kath at Polygon for their endless help and support, and their crucial advice at all stages along the way.

Thanks are also due to Astrid for her support during those first tentative attempts at editing and reading the manuscripts and to all my friends and family who have survived one crisis of self-confidence after another. Acknowledgement must also go to Iona McGregor who agreed despite numerous misgivings to write the introduction at short notice. Thanks also go to my partner Nessa, for everything.

Introduction

IONA MCGREGOR

IN GENRE, style and content this second anthology of gay and lesbian writing ranges as widely as the first, reflecting the fact that homosexual experience is as diverse and contradictory as any other. Individuality was not a popular stance during the embattled 60s and 70s, when a necessary part of the campaign for our rights was to present a united front. Today, we can take a more relaxed attitude. Irreconcilable differences are part of the full human ticket, and getting these across is an important counterbalance to the homophobic stereotypes still propagated by the media.

As with the previous volume, *The Crazy Jig* includes newcomers who are appearing in print for the first time beside long-established writers. The editor is to be congratulated on achieving an even-handed mix of male and female contributors.

No one will be surprised that many of the poems and stories make use of non-Scottish settings. Our national tendency to diaspora has resulted in a high proportion of poets and story-tellers whose talents are set to work on experience gained furth of Scotland. However, it is vital to our culture that the emigrants' road should carry a two-way traffic. The Scottish gay community has played a full part in this process, as can be seen in a selection enriched by contributions from gay black writers born in Scotland and others who have chosen to settle here and take on a Scottish identity.

The reader will find some looks at the outside world where the writers' gayness is merely implied or given a brief mention. This raises some interesting queries: are there any characteristics that distinguish such an unemphasised perspective from that of a 'straight' writer? What is the nature of a gay perspective? Is it any longer possible to define or circumscribe gay writing? Must gay writers assert their identity in order to avoid being deconstructed into the heterosexual majority?

Despite its variety, certain general themes can be discerned in the anthology. Love — always a main topic of lyric verse — is celebrated or mourned. The emotions prompting Edwin Morgan's 'Earl's Court' and 'Tram-Ride, 1939' are echoed by other writers. A line from 'Such A Smile' supplied the title of the collection. In lighter vein, 'Dinner, 7.30 for 8' amusingly blends culinary delights with those to follow, and the trilogy of 'What Lesbians Do ...' debunks the kind of prurient speculation so wearisomely familiar to us from the tabloid press.

Many of the contributions, both verse and prose, strike a sombre note. This is only to be expected. The barriers of isolation and silence may have fallen, but macho male conditioning and the pressure exerted on women to marry continue to distort the public's view of homosexuality. As a consequence, self-oppression is alive and well in our late 20th century. There are gay people of all ages who still find it difficult to admit their true personal needs. How protracted and even painful this rite of passage can be is demonstrated in 'An Exile's Tale' and 'A Sunday Walk'.

'When did you first realise?' remains a question of endless interest to homosexuals. (The final seal of equality will be the freedom to ask 'When did you first realise you were heterosexual?') Self-exploration leads back to childhood and an attempt to make sense of the conflicting aspects of one's own background and personality. In different ways 'Birth Certificate', 'Family Matter', 'A Video of My Father' and 'Travelling' all try to deal with the unabsorbed experience of family history.

In 'Ashes' the narrator links a boyhood memory of his gay uncle's funeral with the more recent death of friends struck down by AIDS, which is also the grim topic of 'From a Diary' and 'The Love that Dare Not'.

Lighter and more humorous contributions also find their place. The text accompanying a recent exhibition of lesbian photography ('Stolen Glances') urged gay artists to colonise heterosexual modes and imagery for their own use. This strategy has already been exploited by our dramatists and fiction writers, and some sharp-edged examples are found in the anthology. One of Hollywood's finest is neatly lassoed in 'Adventurer'; dawning (homo)sexuality becomes Kelmanesque and is given the *parliamo* treatment in 'Monopoly'; a blackly comic murder disposes of a rival in 'Breathtaking Ignorance'.

Perhaps it is inevitable that these excursions emerge as wit and irony rather than the 'layer upon layer of suffering and joy' described by one contributor. (Compared with the lengthy development of heterosexual literary tradition, both feminist fiction and serious gay writing are recent forms). Nevertheless, deeper matters can be glimpsed beneath the wry humour, even if more obliquely offered than in the biographical sketches and poems. The pastiche romanticism of 'Life's Little Loafer' not only resurrects a dead gay author but reminds us, as Edwin Morgan pointed out in his introduction to the previous anthology, that even what there is of our literature has largely been stolen from us and remains hidden. To restore it is as important a task as the publicising of modern gay writing.

The titles I have given illustrate what I see as the main

themes of the anthology. This is not to suggest any ranking order among the contributions or lack of excellence in those not mentioned. I enjoyed every item in the *The Crazy Jig*.

Such A Smile

ALASTAIR S. MACMILLAN

A long time since such a smile
glowed on me.
A pleasure to dance,
and watch clear eyes concentrate
on the crazy jig.
At any time,
a pleasure to dance with such a smile.

Excerpt from Sksuhno

TONI DAVIDSON

THE TRAIN jolted and our bodies touch. A strange and brief caress. Hours before, the touch had been more deliberate, more considered as we searched for new places to turn our bodies electric, hives of live wires. He looked across at me my love and gazed down at our legs still touching from the accidental contact. He didn't take his leg away, neither did I. We let it remain an accident, a trigger to our thoughts which rattled in our heads as our bodies rattled in the train.

We'll be there soon.

I nodded and could think of nothing else to say. The countryside was a bland concoction of brown and green; incongruous farmhouses and flat opaque-coloured villas adorned with terracotta and television aerials. They caught my eye because I cast out for distraction from my thoughts and from the stiffness in my leg which had held its position beyond the accidental contact. There was reassurance in our bones pressing together through rough jeans, there were signs of so much in that aching contact. His needs and mine touching through layers worn and constructed. I had a sense of travel, of leaving one place to arrive in another which didn't imply home or destination. The train hurtling through the suburbs of Paris could have been taking us anywhere from anywhere. It could have been done alone or in different company. Still, our legs were touching and the sensation was something more than physical.

We arrived in St. Lazare early in the morning. Blearily eyed commuters rushed their way down the platform while we lugged rucksacks on to our backs and breathed in secondhand Gauloise smoke. We had arrived here but there were no plans, only, the whim to leave our home behind and replace the urban sprawl with another.

Coffee first.

Yes.

In my paranoia I felt he didn't want to be here. Maybe he'd thought about the destination all the way or maybe already his thoughts were of home, of a familiar bustle of life.

Where?

I don't mind. I don't know.

There is somewhere. I don't know if it's still there or even if it's open but it's good.

There, then.

Disinfectant coated the steps that we took down to the metro. I thought I might slip on their slimy surface and he read my pensive thoughts.

See Paris, break a leg.

As we sat in the train I waited for a jolt and even positioned my leg so that it could easily, deliberately touch his. Typical. From home to destination I was still manufacturing dreams, too impatient to wait their fateful arrival, too hungry for a food I couldn't describe. The metro wound its way through meandering tunnels with scarcely a sideways movement and our legs remained separate, rigid as though suddenly we couldn't move.

In the cafe, on the Marais, the twin spires of Notre Dame

just visible above the houses and pensions, we did our best not to make plans.

What do you want to do here?

Look around, eat and drink and dance and fuck.

Home from home.

Wherever I lay my heart, home is where ...

He smiled, his thin pale lips cracking despite his hands attempting to smother the grin. I was better than he was, I could crack inappropriate and pertinent metaphors all the time without my expression changing. Eventually he always smiled after playing for a while. He stopped me from going insane, prevented my own clever words from choking me. At night when he held me, he put his soft lips to mine and pressed hard as though he was trying to glue my mouth shut and stop the bile from oozing out. But cracks always appeared, they always do.

Later, we sat by the Seine on concrete slabs amongst Parisiens feeling white and foreign. The best feeling I thought. We were without home or destination, no plans had been made, no sightseeing completed. He stretched out beside me and closed his eyes, screwing them shut to make the screen inside darker against the burning sun. I lay down beside him, propping myself up with one elbow bared to the sun. We could have been anywhere. In the flat, in the winter, in the haze, the smog, the arctic air, a heaving throng beside us, teeming sellers of ivory tusks, women with many skirts thrusting bowls into our faces. We could have been there or anywhere. But without home or destination we were beside the Seine hearing boats crawl along the river and the cries of children and radios becoming distant.

Shall we just stay here and not move.

Nomads incarcerated.

Not move, not go, not walk or travel.

You're making plans.

No, I'm not. I'm replacing them.

With what?

Nothing.

He sighed, the air whistling through his pursed lips and he stretched them into a smile. With his eyes closed, I let myself smile fully with no trace of irony, no specks of cynicism. I put my hand on his thin, sinewy thigh and watched the outline of his cock fall against his leg, I moved my hand to his chest and felt, through the thin material his heart beating slowly and as I moved my hand to trace his lips with my fingers, my arm still resting lightly on his chest, I could feel it skip into a faster rhythm.

What Lesbians Do In Jenners

SUSAN MATASOVSKA

The first thing,
Is to sample the perfume.
We tried *égoiste*
And liked its orangeness
(*Aqua Manda*
At six times the price),
Different on thee
And me.
Kiss in the lift
Between floors,
Hold hands in the coats department
Because the big yin's feart
Of the hole in the middle.

What Lesbians Do In The Bath

Susan Matasovska

Prove Archimedes' Principle,
Put toes in naughty places
By way of experiment,
Scrub backs
For each other
And roar with the
Sheer enjoyment of it,
Holding on to the taps,
Cover each other in bubbles
And kiss
Soapily
Before they go to work
On the real business
of the day
Which is managing
To live on each side of the hills
Without digging a tunnel
Through.

What Lesbians Do In Bed

SUSAN MATASOVSKA

Redesign the dachshund (six legs),
Have a fat belly competition
(Hers won, in spite of my sometime lodger),
Visit Africa in the atlas
(Tanzania in particular —
the one-time home of a friend)
Research tides and the phases of the moon
In the encyclopaedia,
Do the crossword
In between passion and lust
(which were quite nice)
Redraw the edge of things;
Since our reality
Is no longer theirs,
We must establish
Our own.

The Ballad of the Tabla Player

Ronnie Walsh

DURING the monsoon rains lightning played around the
column of the Gulábi Minár (the pink minaret), illuminating The Word of God. The abstract calligraphy, so stylised
that no one could hope to decipher it, stood naked and
vulnerable against the night sky. Ásha was naturally at-
tuned to such phenomena and was quick to draw the in-
ference; the Body was indeed profane — only The Word
was real. Distant Brihaspáti and Sháni were as specks of
dust, perhaps Jupiter and Saturn *were* mere specks of dust
in some other more certain, more logical world. Perhaps the
thinker left only his thoughts behind as evidence of his
existence to be recalled by another self at some other identical moment in time. Perhaps, perhaps ... This word
seemed to Ásha the most sincere.

RAAM NAAM SUCH HAI! God's Name is Truth. This, the
morning's procession had proclaimed as Hóli was celebrated
with the vivid colours of menstruation. But what then are we?
A lie? If so, then we deceive ourselves because we cannot live
with The Truth. In the same way that we cannot follow the
course of the sun at his zenith. We find Beauty only in the dying
sunset, we need Uncertainty. Ásha let the night enfold her and
remained motionless until the rain had cleansed her of the
caked powders. A warm pool collected at her feet and from
within came the lure of a flute. Súraj was improvising a
midnight raga and his friend's tabla seemed to echo her
heartbeat. Flute and heart were momentarily One.

Once inside, she met fully her betrothed's steady gaze. The menfolk must already have been fed since her mother was eating róti. This was tradition only, they were a liberal family and Ásha had grown up familiar with choice; Súraj would certainly have been her first choice, he was so fair with his unexpected green eyes. Both young people were medical students and everyone had agreed that their marriage would be a success. They waited only for the announcement of that auspicious day when they would both circle the fire while the priest intoned the Holy Védas. Rice, the symbol of fertility, would be cast on the fire. Rice cannot bear grain until it has been transplanted. Ásha would be transplanted to her husband's family, she would be fruitful and faithful — the fire is also a reminder.

Their wedding day dawned bleak and overcast. The ceremony itself went without omen, the happy couple thrice circling the holy flame, but afterwards Súraj's mother was heard by the whole company to argue violently with Ramésh, Súraj's friend. Since she spoke only Kashmíri, no one could ascertain what the cause of the argument had been. Ásha felt a vague foreboding and as she stepped into the palanquin to be escorted to her new home, the rain began to extinguish the joss sticks which she held in her hand. The henna and dyes painstakingly used to draw spiral patterns over her palms began to stain the sleeves of her dress.

Her mother-in-law wasn't envious of her beauty or vindictive toward her or even cruel — she just ignored her. They had no linking language between them, but Ásha suspected that even if they had, the woman's attitude would have been the same.

Súraj once made her the gift of a god. Before their marriage he had presented her with Hánuman, and now during his long absences she consoled herself by trying to form sentences out of the monkey's inane chatter. This god was also a thief: he would steal betel nuts from the huge copper storage pots which she filled every morning. By Zohár (the afternoon call to prayer), the monkey's lips would be stained scarlet. Such little things made her life tolerable.

Súraj had gone to Srínagar with his friend. The pines and mosses not only looked green, they felt green. Green beyond human vanity. Súraj's mind turned verdant. For no reason at all the word 'Adolescentia' became his thought. Not just Youth as a quality fixed in time, but growing youthful eternally. He sensed the spirit of the mountains, a scent so astringent as to banish Putrescence, even the memory of putrescence forever. Súraj was happy.

'Mi amador tiene los ojos azules — azul como el mar!' My lover has blue eyes, as blue as the sea. The new housemaid sings in Spanish. Esperança comes from Goa and speaks both Portuguese and Spanish. When her work is done, Esperança joins Ásha in the garden enclosure where they pick flowers and dry spices together. The task is wholesome and since Ásha has given up her studies, she welcomes the opportunity to learn two more European languages. Ásha is happy.

When Ásha and Súraj next met, they met as strangers. Súraj's mother hovered over them like a vulture over carrion. Esperança plied them with sweetmeats and Hánuman could not decide which of the pair to climb over.

'Súraj, you mustn't go gallivanting with that boy, you have a duty here. Spending your honeymoon with a Chandála (dog-eater / casteless person). Has anyone yet heard of such a thing!' Súraj's mother speaks to him in Kashmíri.

'Esperança, don't look so guilty, you'll drop that tray if you're not careful. We've done nothing to be ashamed of!' Ásha speaks to Esperança in Spanish.

'Námaste! I bow to you. Námaste! I bow to you.' (The Formal Salutation). Ásha and Súraj speak to each other. Súraj in English says 'Ásha we must talk privately. I think we know each other's mind and I do care for you.'

'Is it then so obvious? Our families will never allow it and there is the dowry to be considered, and the family line.'

'We can adopt a child in Srínagar. I shall be working there and you and the maid will join us. Your letters were full of her ...'

'And yours of the tabla player.'

'They have no respect for us, why should we feel guilty? This way four people can be happy and a child will have a home.'

'It is a life of deception you propose.'

'It is the only life we are allowed.'

'By the law?'

'By Tradition.'

The four lovers lived on a houseboat moored to the shore of Lake Dal. Esperança from the tropical South and Ásha from the plains had never before seen the colours of autumn or the pale snow. After a year, when they guessed it was safe, Súraj acquired a newborn child, their 'firstborn'. The grandparents were prevented from attending the birth by the seasonal winter snows. All seemed perfect.

When rumours reached Hakím, a doctor of Islamic law, that a Moslem child had been purchased by Hindús he set out to investigate. Kashmír is predominantly Moslem, but with a Hindu ruling class. The country has been at the heart of many of the fratricidal disputes between Pakistan and India. When Hakím learned of the unsavoury disposition of the persons involved, (the tabla player was a known Gándhu), he roused the local people. The two women were spat upon whenever they went to the bazaar to buy provisions. Even the tabla player, who had hitherto been a popular if marginal member of the community, was beaten with lathees (staves). For once, the local Moslems and Hindús found themselves united.

SÚRAJ: 'We must give up the child. They will only take her back in any case.'

ÁSHA: 'Take her back to what? The mob won't feed her.'

SÚRAJ: 'Soon we shall have no money to feed even ourselves. I too dreamt of having a second child in a few years time, but now that we have lost our firstborn, we cannot return to Delhi.'

ÁSHA: 'I wouldn't want to go back there.'

SÚRAJ: 'Where will you go?'

ÁSHA: 'With Esperança, if she will have me. We can both work in the South and try to earn enough money there to go abroad. And you?'

SÚRAJ: 'I'll go with Ramésh. Doctors and tabla players are always in demand. I couldn't foresee that it would turn out this way. We were happy and I love you, wife.'

ÁSHA: 'I love you Súraj. In another life we shall again be husband and wife, and Esperança and Ramésh will be our lovers.'

SÚRAJ: 'But we shall not know ourselves!'

ÁSHA: 'Will that matter?'

SÚRAJ: 'No.'

Ásha and Esperança eventually made it to Lisbon where Esperança began work as a model. Súraj died of consumption in the slums of Calcutta. The tabla player, alas, cannot be traced.

Dinner, 7.30 for 8

ANDREW STAFFORD

6:20, egg whites, oven on,
I'm in love, Blond, Blue Eyes.
Lamb's lettuce (mâche), two ducks, boned,
He's perfect, I'm happy, Blonde,
Thickened veal stock, onion, seasoning,
We met in our Pub, Friday, We laughed,
Clarified Butter, Cream,
Bronski beat, followed by Albinoni,
Deglaze with vinegar, white wine,
Pints of Heavy, Haggis Supper,
Mushrooms thinly sliced, Chutney, Claret,
Hot oil massage in front of the fire,
A little more seasoning,
Warm and soapy shower, dry together,
To bed, drunk with cats,
Arrange on a plate with sauce and garnish,
Like a dream we were, together,
Keep warm until he arrives for dinner.

Table for One

STEVE ANTHONY

Even an avocado's made for two,
sharing itself so openly;

food's version of foreplay,
appetiser to the feast.

As I savour one now, I see you
scooping your favourite fruit

and smiling up at me, happy —
like you were that long afternoon

in some out-of-season hotel,
where we emptied the day of everything

but ourselves, and were satisfied.
I'm left with a hollow skin.

The Single Bed Years

KAY WEST

I REMEMBER the day you called, when I dashed to the 'phone clad in my greens and yelled my news to Tom who happened to be passing that you'd got it, you'd got it! Tom and I danced up the corridor in our white bloodstained clogs and clattered into theatre three only to be frowned upon by Sister Mack as we both sat jubilantly discussing my news. At lunch I'd sat oblivious to everything except my own thoughts, not knowing how I'd survive the month till I'd be with you. Oh and the blissful headache of organising a transfer, of packing and persuading my very sensible father to become a removal firm for an evening. I remember going back to my room in the nurse's home and quelling my immediate need for you and then bells rang and there was your soft northern voice at the end of the line.

So I arrived in the month of September with my father littering your living room with boxes, suitcases and ruck-sacks. You looked on horrified while I tried to persuade you between staff farewell party hiccups that I had indeed tossed out my junk. I stood clutching my handbag, avoiding your penetrating gaze as my father cast curious glances from behind a packing box.

Later, after my father and I had eaten your carefully prepared salad (he was disappointed, he wanted to sample the famous north-east fish supper) and he had retreated to the west coast in his immaculate BMW, we were finally alone and I took you my flatmate, my landlady into my arms. I breathed your exquisite perfume, kissed your aquiline nose and you laid your head on my breast and stared disdainfully at my scattered belongings.

It was late when we finally reached bed, only after you insisted that I unpack and your washing machine accumulated a dozen pairs of dirty denims. You worried that the neighbours would think that a man had moved in when they saw them on the washing-line the next day.

Oh but lady! Blue eyes! The bed! I could not conceal my disappointment when a single bed blinded my vision and you stood naked apart from your mini briefs and insisted it was the largest single bed in town. I asked if you had taken a tape measure as you bashfully explained the shopping trip with your ageing mother, who was after all paying for this piece of treasured furniture, the assistant's confusion as you had said a double, your mother a single and the assistant's wicked snigger as your mum demanded the reason for your need of a double bed. Blue eyes, I could envisage it all as your face became the colour of the plush maroon carpet. You said the single bed would be cosier for us and I agreed as we hurriedly satiated our passion and then you added that we'd have the rest of our lives as you saw me quizzically glance at the mere quarter hour that had passed on the clock. I had slept dreaming about the rest of our lives in a single bed.

A couple of months passed. We settled into a routine like newly weds. We argued over the housework. I cooked while you dusted every speck of dust you could find and deplored my nicotine habit which was to your way of thinking increasing your amount of chores. Yet we shared our baths, our passions and tins of lager and packets of peanuts and watched the soap operas. I introduced you to literature and chilli con carne while you went to work on my wardrobe and appointed yourself my personal accountant.

I met your family, introduced as your flatmate of course, and your straight friends whom I instantly disliked. We entertained gay couples with cheap liebfraumilch and chilli and discussed the gossip of the week. You'd trail guests round your new flat, briefly stopping in 'your' bedroom as the heterosexuals admired the decor and the homosexuals gazed amazedly at the single bed.

Winter arrived and with it my family for a tour of inspection under the guise of my birthday. We hurriedly made a makeshift bedroom out of the boxroom installing a z-bed and some of my junk, then you sat and worried. I puffed languidly on my cigarette, unearthed my moussaka recipe, vexed I would be unable to spend my birthday night with you.

I will never forget my mother's arrival as she swept past your astonished face and conducted her own tour. She peered out the kitchen window, stopped off in the loo before she entered 'your' bedroom at which she disinterestedly glanced round. She flung open the door to 'my' bedroom and stopped short while I had flung the door back with a comment of 'just my usual mess, mum!'

Do you remember how relieved we were when they left and we sank thankfully into our single bed? We stretched its springs as we stretched our bodies and you tried to smother my passions with the pillow for fear the deaf old lady next door would hear. I still laugh as I recall your stunned expression when I expounded another of my 'they must know' theories. I reminded you of the same single sheet, pillowcase and kingsize continental quilt cover which hung faithfully every fortnight on the communal green to dry in a billowy north-east wind.

A year or so passed. We continued to share our lives, our baths, our passions and the single bed. Holidays were spent in twin-bedded hotel rooms with the customary half hour employed energetically crumpling the sheets of the unused bed before a maid knocked on the door. Christmas arrived once again and we showered each other with gifts expensive and not so expensive. We cooked our own turkey, drank French red wine and retired to the single bed early. I remember sitting inebriated at your family Christmas dinner, tossing off liqueurs while you apprehensively watched my every move and evaluated my conversation. I watched your uninhibited delight as you unwrapped your presents and almost kicked myself as I nearly thanked your sister for giving you an electric blanket (single size of course!)

Months later we weren't on speaking terms as I impulsively indulged my maternal instincts and bought a dog and changed our comfortable lives overnight. I had tried to persuade you that it was easier than my having a baby. You had sat aghast and distressed as you sought for the plausible answer to your family's imminent question of how you, the landlady, could allow your headstrong flatmate to bring a dog into your home. Luckily they were charmed by her, just as you were and you came to love her despite the puddles that appeared on the carpet.

We were a family now and we shared our lives with our little friend, our home, our food, our packets of peanuts and the single bed. In the morning when she woke she'd bound through to the bedroom and with a leap like a high jumper she'd land across your shoulders and you'd curse and grunt and tell me I should take her walkies even though it was only five a.m. Instead I'd try and squeeze her into the remaining available space.

Blue eyes, believe me when I say I cursed too as I'd try and pull your warm body closer while the dog wriggled between us and fought for her share of the pillow. Amorous a.m.'s were evicted from our lives and the bed linen was promoted to a weekly wash.

It all got too much in the end. We both woke with aching muscles and stiff spines as the single bed refused two adults sprawling space. We argued over the unthinkable — buying a double bed as we lay in our single but couldn't think of a suitable excuse. We thought a double bed too obvious and you argued that our personal comfort was a selfish consideration. Think of how hurt your family would be when truth met their eyes as they saw 'your' new bed. We somehow actually reached the stage of debating who would pay. You pointed out that you had bought the flat and the leather suite. I had to remind you of a recent shopping trip of mine when you sent me out for bread and milk and I had come back with a three-year-old Ford Fiesta acquired on hire purchase. But it was the vision of us both shyly bouncing our buttocks in front of a harassed Saturday salesman and the odd stares from milling shoppers that had us finally rejecting the idea and so we faithfully continued to clamber into the single bed each evening.

Yet I needed time to think so I packed my bags and set off for suburban Glasgow and a week of family quibbles and a concerned father as I hit the city nightspots and staggered in at breakfast time. As was expected I didn't last the week. I upset the household routine and the daily help handed in her notice.

So I arrived home and changed your immaculate flat into chaos once more as I unsuccessfully attempted to unpack my haphazardly packed bags. You expertly and skilfully arranged the loads for the machine and I gave you a present of rock which I knew you would hate and I would eat later.

Yet I had the time to think during my brief holiday and told you that enough was enough and no longer could I tolerate the confines of the single bed and all that it represented of our lives. Something had to change and again we launched into long tedious discussions of double beds, your paranoia and my seeming boldness. The discussion became rage which lasted an hour, with the dog refereeing from under the settee until I slammed out of the flat, the dog whimpering at my heels.

Do you remember, Blue eyes, when I 'phoned you hours later and told you that I'd got it, I'd got it? You snapped back down the static, 'got what?' and slammed the 'phone down. I raced back to the flat and successfully persuaded a very disgruntled you to participate in my mystery tour.

I will never forget the look of amazement on your face as I conducted the tour round the quiet semi that had two double bedrooms, with ample space for two double beds, and a much needed back garden for the dog. Nervously, Blue eyes, I had looked at you, unable to penetrate your business-like stare as you surveyed the property and held up a questioning finger of dust from the window sill. Seconds later your blue eyes had sparkled and smiled and we shook hands on our deal and hurried back to the single bed.

By the end of that summer we had moved and settled into our semi and more importantly our double bed. Yet it wasn't long after that we found ourselves staring at each other across the extra space, gave chaste little kisses and went our sprawling separate ways and slept. And I slept dreaming of the single bed years.

On the Death of Hart Crane

MICHAEL VERINO

Death, here is your son.
   Far to the south, beyond the sandpipers' shrilling,
and the Cuban pines and stars and crocus isles
   fixed fast under Aztec eyes,
he lies, planted, down there
   in that most prolific oblivion of the sea,
the shark gardens, voiceless, down there
   with his topsy-turvy boys in blue
or summer white, anchorless in the tides,
   their hands clutching Carib emeralds,
their eyes dancing like tempests
   like other men's eyes, cloud, wind, and rain;
he loved them, and broke himself on his love,
   on the reef of it, of them,
argonauts of desire, wrecked, down there:
   'The bottom of the sea is cruel.'

Death, here is your son,
   born in Ohio candy commerce,
for whom the city was refuge and shock and temptation:
   first the cornet blazing cryptic flashes
from the dazzled midnight roofs,
   then the stoical faces in the tubes,
shot, trailing quotations like tickertape,
   shot, trailing quotations like bunting

on the Fourth of July bridging Portland and Portland,
    backward to Atlantis, forward to Armageddon.

Death, here is your son
    whose summer went as the smoke goes,
when ships sailed again for Vera Cruz
    and green-eyed sailors sang of Stamboul Rose,
while he took his limbo and washed down
    candy commerce into nightmare;
down there he went for Montezuma, breaking —
    came back from Montezuma, broken, winnowed,
and took that last draught, of the sea;
    under Aztec eyes
he lies, in the sea which is his much-sung-of self,
    singing, 'Sea, take me,
and make me grow above your silence';
    whose song, Death, shares the watery source,
and the waves the wind's new tempi,
    and the sunlight scanning his dithyrambs
in the cusps, sunlight's deep sonority
    growing high as noontide above your silence.

Paper Boy

MICHAEL VERINO

At eighteen he will be
peach-ripe enough
to set any heart dancing ...

Paper boy
shirt-tail flying
his buttocks pressed against
white ducks
smearing his bike seat
with innocent heat —
He's white and fast
delivering the news
along the green streets —
Bombings and horoscopes and ball scores,
the music of the spheres
of influence, the gossip
of the cosmos —
What does he know?
He's too fast to reflect,
or really to be seen
only a streak
of hair
as he splashes through the air —
In the cool green
boring shade,

weddings and graduations
are experience.

There are probably many
who would not want him now.
I'd take him if he's a cast-off.
I'd take the risk.
I wouldn't mind walking hand-in-hand
with him in the woods
or down Main Street.
I would tolerate his imperfections.

For tucked away somewhere
in the best suit of himself
is his little enfolded soul
like the clean, crisp linen handkerchief
he carries to Sunday School
and forgets in his pocket the rest of the week.
I seem to see a corner of it
peeking out of the smile of him
as he flies past,
a mere intimation of it.
I'd like to investigate further,
like to take it by the corner of it I seem to see
and draw it slowly out
over the years till he's eighteen
and my heart's dancing,
and unfold it fully square,
white, unsullied ...

Lesbians and Gays in
the Scottish Republic

GRAEME WOOLASTON

HOW MANY lesbians and gays are there in Scotland? A much-quoted statistic claims that one in ten of the population is gay. Applied to Scotland this produces an estimate of half-a-million people.

I'm afraid I don't believe this for one moment. All the available evidence indicates that we should calculate our numbers very conservatively indeed. In Glasgow there are six hundred licensed outlets, of which five are gay. The capital city sustains two gay bars. Between them Edinburgh and Glasgow at present have five gay discos. The rest of the central belt contains a total of three partly-gay bars. The only one I know well, in Stirling, is overwhelmingly straight.

The aggregate circulation of gay magazines in Scotland is less than five thousand. Since many people buy both *Gay Scotland* and a UK title, the number of purchasers is fewer than that. Allowance has to be made for the fact that this figure is artificially depressed by the refusal of John Menzies, who overwhelmingly control retail outlets in Scotland, to deal in gay titles.

Gay Scotland survives with many difficulties. Its editor has a constant problem in attracting contributions, especially from lesbians. The Scottish Homosexual Rights Group has a membership of just over a hundred. No other non-specialist gay organisation, except those for young people, has ever managed to establish itself in Scotland.

Where, then, are the half-million? They don't drink in gay bars, they don't buy gay magazines, they don't use the cruising grounds, they don't advertise in the personal columns, they don't cottage. Invisible and ineffable indeed.

It is, of course, immensely difficult to judge how many people might be bisexual, or at least married but enjoying gay sex as well. Anecdotal accounts, and experience, suggest that in Scotland this is much more common than south of the Border. But even if a reasonable guess at the numbers of such people is added into the total, I cannot see that gays / lesbians / bisexuals in Scotland are more than tens of thousands. It seems likely that we may be about the same size as the Gaelic-speaking community: 80,000. We are perhaps fewer than that.

In a population of five million this means we are a small minority. But we need not be weak. I make the comparison with Gaelic speakers deliberately, because as a similar minority they are very well organised and extremely efficient in obtaining funding from the Scottish Office and the Scottish Arts Council. Nearly one-fifth of SAC's budget in support of publishing goes to the Gaelic Books Council — a proportion ten times greater than the proportion of Gaelic readers in the population.

What do Gaelic speakers possess that we don't? After all, their language, though temptingly beautiful to listen to, is very difficult to learn, and they are weakest where we are strongest, in the two urban centres of power and wealth in Scotland.

The answer, I would suggest, is that they believe in themselves. They do not question their right to a place in the Scottish sun. They are convinced — in my view, rightly — that any conceivable future Scotland, independent or otherwise, will owe something of its character to their contribution to its life and culture.

This kind of self-confidence is what we need, and we clearly don't have.

There are, it seems to me, some very intriguing parallels between being Scottish and being lesbian or gay. Both are minority experiences sustained in the face of a massive hegemonic presence: heterosexuality, English domination of the Union. (Let me make it clear that I am not indulging here in that most pathetic of all the vices of a non-independent Scotland, Anglophobia. The English don't dominate the Union out of some obscure malice. It's a simple question of arithmetic: they are nine times more numerous than we are.)

To be gay, as to be Scottish, is to doubt yourself. The single most depressing statistic about Scotland is that less than 40% of Scots support independence. After half-a-century of the national movement, after a surge of political and cultural awareness which has swept forward throughout the past twenty years, more than six out of ten Scots still don't believe that their country either can or should be free.[1]

This is the inevitable result of three centuries of believing that where we are different from England, we are inferior. We have abandoned the Scots language to the point where it is almost beyond hope of revival. We have been repeatedly told that our accents are comic, incomprehensible, or at best, 'regional'. The worst wound of all has been self-inflicted: the wretched influence, which cannot be too strongly deprecated, of a form of Christianity which emphasises the negative features of that

[1]   As this book goes to press, some opinion polls have begun to suggest a sudden rise in support for independence. If this trend is maintained, perhaps my comments on Scottish self-doubt will soon be out of date.

faith and denies any liturgical lifting-up of the human spirit.

It is well known that Scots compensate for their in-feriority complex by absurd gestures of misplaced emotionalism, such as celebrating England's defeat by Germany in the World Cup by singing 'Deutschland über Alles' while bedecked in tartan. We cherish the myth that we are a proud, aggressive people, so proud and aggressive that when, in 1979, we were offered a very limited measure of self-government, we promptly crapped our national pants.

Similarly, we lesbians and gays lack an essential element of self-belief. This, again, is not surprising, for it is only in the last twenty years that the view has been widely propagated that we *ought* to have self-belief. I can still remember the first occasions when I encountered in print, at the age of maybe eighteen or nineteen, the opinion that there was nothing wrong in being homosexual. I can still remember the shock it gave me, and then the growing, tantalising sense of a whole new possible way of living.

Lesbians and gays generally, not just in Scotland, tend to lie low and keep quiet about themselves. This gay habit of silence even seems to extend towards their own press. It's notoriously difficult to stimulate the readership of the gay press into answering back or responding to features or expressions of opinion. It's as if the gay instinct to keep mum is so ingrained it can't even be broken within the confines of our own community. (The only occasions I have had noticeable reader response to material in *Gay Times* is when I've written about football. I now suspect that it's more dangerous to express an opinion about football in *Gay Times* than to express an opinion about homosexuality in the *Church Times*.)

We Scottish lesbians and gays are plagued by a double *damnosa hereditas* of self-doubt. Within a nation nervous about asserting its rights, we belong to a minority which is everywhere nervous about asserting its rights. Among a tongue-tied people we are tongue-tied still further: trained as Scots to think of ourselves as culturally second-best, and trained as gays to think of ourselves as psychologically second-best.

And just as the Scots compensate for their self-doubt by ferocious assertiveness on the crumbling terraces of Hampden, we lesbians and gays compensate by grossly exaggerating our numbers within the community as a whole.

But though it's easy enough to analyse the problem, Heaven knows what the answer is. How do you give self-confidence to adults who haven't acquired it naturally through the process of growing up? It's very difficult to achieve this with an individual, let alone a whole community, as anyone can testify who has known, for example, a bisexual still unable in maturity to accept the gay component of their sexuality.

How do you give pride to a people? The identical dilemma faces the gay rights activist and the Scottish nationalist. A partial answer, of course, lies in books such as this. One area of Scottish gay life which is encouragingly alive and kicking is artistic self-expression, especially by younger writers. An outstanding example, though not the only one, is Clyde Unity Theatre, who have brilliantly learned to use a populist tradition of comedy, with a recognisable derivation from music hall and even from 'The Broons', as a vehicle for upfront, radical sexual politics. Another encouraging sign is the increase in activism amongst young lesbians and gays, especially in Glasgow, where they are the driving-force behind the attempt to set up a Glasgow Lesbian and Gay Centre. In many ways they seem the natural heirs of those of us who were involved in the early gay movement about the time they were born. (The intervening age-group, I'm afraid, appears to have regarded growing a moustache as the limit of its commitment to the gay cause.)

But the fundamental problem still remains, that the normal, everyday experience of lesbian and gay life in Scotland is hedged in by self-created, or at least self-sustained, fears. I came back to Scotland five years ago after a long time in England, and I am still sometimes taken aback to discover an inability simply to come to terms with being gay which I had thought was a thing of the past, at least among people younger than myself. In Scotland it isn't. And our Scottishness shows itself in other ways which are disturbing. I've compared notes with people who have similarly returned from the south, and we are agreed that simple prudery, a basic sense of shame about the body, is an extraordinary surviving feature of modern Scotland. It really is bizarre to listen to gay men in an all-male household expressing genuine outrage when someone casually wanders around in the nude, or to encounter a man in his thirties who doesn't want to undress in your sight, or to see gay men in the Gents of a gay bar go to the cubicles for a piss rather than the urinals — the most extraordinary manifestation of *pudeur* I have ever witnessed anywhere. All of this is a reflection of a phenomenon which extends far beyond the lesbian and gay community: a nation where the swimming-pools have signs asking people to keep their costumes on in single-sex showers is a nation with a problem.

But it is, of course, peripheral to the central problem of Scotland: how to make this frustrating, exasperating, confused, tiresome, irresistible country of ours have enough faith in itself to claim its right to full self-government. As the title of this piece indicates, I want to see us progress to the creation of a Scottish Republic. I believe that when we extricate ourselves from the decaying body politic of the United Kingdom we should simultaneously free ourselves of the increasingly tacky House of Windsor (with the exception of the Duchess of Rothesay[1], whom lesbians and gays will always have cause to make welcome).

The philosophy of a republic is that it consists, not of the subjects of a monarch, but of a commonwealth of equal citizens. Basing our claim on this fundamental principle, we lesbians and gays would insist on *our* place in the Scottish Republic, equal in the eyes of its laws and in recognition by its public bodies. But to win this right in any conceivable self-governing Scotland, even one with only limited freedom, we have to stake our claim now. It isn't going to drop from Heaven like manna. Nor should it. If we haven't the gumption to stand up for ourselves, we don't deserve equality.

To counter the miasma of doubts and misgivings which can always threaten to descend like the famous mists of our land we should repeat to ourselves as if it were a mantra: Scotland must be free, and lesbians and gays must be free within it.

1   The Scottish title of Princess Diana.

Serge Into Silk

JOANNE WINNING

She weaves her fabric of tomorrow
Into the cloth of my being.
She fits today.
She clothes yesterday.
Under her bridge
The dead wood of autumn has flowed.
All is new in my valley.

The Weaver my Lover
On the loom of my body
Has made
Rough into Smooth
Today into Tomorrow
Serge into Silk.

As long as I am taken

JOANNE WINNING

There you are,
A thousand miles away from me across our bedroom.
(Working late while I chase sleep)
Tossing figures and sculpting science.
Sitting in an ochred glow —
All sexy silhouette.

Your head is bent against the challenge.
Your eyes are locked into the page.
Every feature, from nose to cheek,
Intent upon the buffeting chaos.
It is a hard face — a working face.

But also there, the face that many many times
Has risen suddenly above me in the night,
Out of another world.
Bearing a beautiful woman's body
Down upon my own.
An urgent, passionate, pleading face.

And then, as if the double vision
Had collected in one place,
I see two faces in one,
Chiming in time with each other —
Duality in every line.

So.
Are you Lover or Scientist?
...

Here I lie,
Crazy to know.
Transfixed by the light from you,
outshining the lamp.
Wondering whose eyes would turn on me now,
Breathless and all Willingness
To be seduced
Or to be intellectualised
As long as I am taken.

Birth Certificate

MAYA CHOWDHRY

My birth certificate says
born in Edinburgh, Scotland, 1964
but I was born in the world
and the year doesn't matter.

Born of the blood of more than
one race, I live my life as two
in a country that doesn't accept
birthplace as race
and race as place of birth.

Seventeen years of denials that
two halves make a whole
the past nine were spent untying
knots I tied up my feelings with
to stop them tearing apart.

Unpicking the tangled
vision I had of
an Indian / Scots girl
in a long red skirt and bangles
on trains between Edinburgh and London
in search of a place of rest,
two days and nights
on the Rajdani express.

Travelling, looking for an image of
A Scots / Indian girl
in a red shalwaar kameez and shoes
asking you in broken Hindi the way home.
Kahaa hai?

She was an illusion,
couldn't find her
veils in temples of twenty-seven states
covering my eyes
Six times she bled
in her months of travelling
and six times I asked her
where her blood belonged
which faces in the crowd matched hers
which earth would swallow her
which was the land of her birth.

Ashes

KENNEDY WILSON

JUNE, 1973

'IT WAS a great turn out,' said Logan's father as if they were returning from a football match.

'I only hope I have as many people to my burial,' said Logan's mother.

'It wasn't a burial, it was a burning,' muttered Logan from the back of the car.

'Don't be disrespectful. Your uncle was a good man.'

The family car swung up the short drive of the bungalow. Inside, other family members had gathered for pale sherry, tea, shortbread and little sandwiches with the crusts cut off. Logan was plainly bored. This was an anticlimax after the sight of his first coffin and the weird way it slid away behind royal blue velvet curtains to unknown ovens beyond.

Suddenly the wake, if that's what it was, looked up. Not only had Logan skilfully avoided the vermilion kisses of his Aunt Kathleen but he had seen his cousin Mark who, a few years older, was bursting with post-pubescent promise.

'Hi, Mark,' said Logan, slyly eyeing the older boy's slim flanks.

'Hi,' he cooly replied.

'What did you think of the burning?' asked Logan.

'The what?'

'You know, the crematorium,' he hissed.

'Is this your first death?' Mark asked. 'I've been to funerals before.'

Logan decided to change tack. 'You know what they say about Uncle Jim,' he said conspiratorially.

'What?'

'Didn't you see those old men at the service? Uncle Jim's cronies. Camp as a row of tents most of them.'

'Are you saying that Uncle Jim was a bachelor gay?' asked Mark.

Logan nodded with authority.

'Well, it doesn't make you a bad person!' Mark added, cocking his eyebrow in a way Logan didn't quite understand. Mark fished in his pockets and pulled out a packet of cigarettes. Logan gasped audibly.

'Do your parents allow you to smoke?' he asked astonished.

'Parent,' he said clicking the final *t*. 'My parents are divorced.'

'I think I'd like to be cremated when I go,' said Logan smirking.

'Your ashes scattered to the four winds ...'

'Yeah, from a helicopter.'

APRIL, 1988

'Nope, there's a West Virginia, but no such thing as an East Virginia,' said Ben as he drove Logan across the West Virginia / Maryland state line. Their destination was an old house where a memorial get-together was being held for Frank, a friend of Ben's who had died in January.

It wasn't to be a formal or a dismal affair. Frank's parents had cruelly insisted on not having a funeral service of any kind and his friends and former lovers had not had a chance to say goodbye. The guests were bringing flowers to plant in the garden. It was a mild day but a strong breeze was whipping at the clouds and rain threatened. It was what Ben called 'sweater weather'.

Logan had met Ben less than a year before while waiting in a queue at a London theatre. They fell into conversation and spent a couple of days together before Ben flew back to the States. They'd written to each other ever since. Finally Logan had decided to visit Ben and see something of his home town, Baltimore, and nearby Washington DC.

The party (that was what it was) was held in the garden. Spring buds were pushing into leaf and the first blossoms were visible on the cherry trees. There were about twenty men there when Ben and Logan arrived, along with a few women.

Tables were spread with chintzy cloths, big bunches of grapes and sprays of flowers, along with plates of sandwiches and canapés. 'Tony's never been the same since he started doing the windows of Laura Ashley,' Logan overheard someone say.

Ben introduced Logan to a few people who were intrigued by his Scottish accent. One was a landscape gardener who had been to Scotland on a study-tour and knew the gardens at Culzean Castle and Inverewe, and the Edinburgh Botanics. There was a queeny older guy who had flown in from New York, two attractive men who obviously spent too much time in the gym and the acidly witty Tony who brazenly sought compliments on his extravagant table displays. It's true, thought Logan, gays are the same the world over!

Logan was expecting some sort of speech but nothing materialised. Slowly people wandered over to a large flowerbed and knelt with their plants. Logan was moved as old friends remembered Frank and hugged each other. Some were slightly damp-eyed but the afternoon did not turn maudlin.

As the crowd gathered at the flower bed to see their handiwork a sudden gust billowed the chintz tablecloths, and several glasses were knocked over and smashed. Heavy spots of rain fell. 'That'll be Frank,' said Tony.

Around three in the afternoon Logan got into Ben's VW Fox and they pulled away from the house with a toot and a wave. 'I don't suppose you realised,' said Ben, 'but seventy-five per cent of the guys there are HIV-positive.'

NOVEMBER, 1990

Wintery rain lashed the brightly anoraked walkers as they trudged up a hillside above a small Borders town. This wasn't Logan's idea of a fun day out. Normally he'd spend his Sundays lounging around and reading the papers.

Today was different. He had agreed to come never imagining that the weather would be this bad. Bitingly cold wind accompanied driving rain. But he could hardly say that he'd just sit in the car while the others made the trek to the top. This was not just a day out. They had come to scatter Paul's ashes.

Paul was hardly a close friend but he was the first person Logan had known who had died of AIDS. Indeed, this was his first contemporary who had died since the school 'bad girl' had been killed in a car crash in Arran. The teachers had always said that no good would come of her.

As the weather worsened Logan began not to notice it. It was exhilarating in an odd way. When they reached the top of the mountain Paul's brother produced a box which contained the ashes. Logan thought that they'd be sprinkled like seeds sown in a biblical garden. But the bag was bigger than he imagined and while some of the grey ash was carried off by the wind a lot of it plopped unceremoniously to the ground.

Paul was a kind man, well-liked, intelligent, thoughtful. He was almost Logan's age and it made him think of his own mortality. 'Why him?' Logan thought as he was handed a paper cup of Glenmorangie by one of the anoraks.

The group huddled silently together, their heads uncovered. 'Whisky never tasted so good as on top of a mountain,' someone said. As Logan sipped, the rain hid his tears.

Life's Little Loafer
An Old Story Rediscovered

Hubert Kennedy

When my dear friend Ian returned recently from a holiday in Germany, he gave me the manuscript of the following story. At first I did not appreciate its possible origin, for it was in English, not German. He himself did not know where it had come from; it was given him by someone he met casually in Berlin. He had mentioned my name by chance, and his new acquaintance said that he knew of my interests and asked him to give the manuscript to me, remarking only that he thought I would enjoy reading it. It had no title and no author was named, but my interest was aroused by the very first sentence, for it appeared to be a translation of a story by the Scottish-German anarchist writer John Henry Mackay. My first impression was confirmed again and again as I read on, so that by the time I had finished there was no doubt in my mind that Mackay had written it. But where was the original? I quizzed Ian about it, but he was no help. Forgetful as ever, Ian could not even recall the man's name. But let me explain why I feel so certain of the authorship of the story.

Although Mackay was born in Greenock, after the early death of his Scottish father his mother took him back to her native Germany, where he grew up speaking German. In 1896 he wrote a charming story that he called 'The Sybarite'. The title character is named Germann and the story tells of the narrator's meeting with him in Geneva and the evening they spent together. Near the beginning of the story, as the two are leaving the Taverne Anglaise where they have dined, Germann introduces the narrator (clearly Mackay himself) to a young man named Astruc cadet. At this

point the narrator interrupts the story with the following paren-
thesis:

> (How could I have guessed that I would later write both their
> stories! For one day I will also describe Astruc, life's little loafer,
> whom later that evening my new friend incidentally called a
> Sybarite of Freedom and a Complete Anarchist ...)

Despite this promise, the character Astruc never showed up
again in any of Mackay's stories. I had supposed that, pressed by
other matters, Mackay had simply abandoned the idea of writing
Astruc's tale. And yet, here it was! On reflection, the reason for
its apparent suppression by Mackay became clear. If he had
published it under the pseudonym Sagitta (which he used for his
various writings on man / boy love), or even anonymously, it
would have been immediately recognized that the author of this
story was also the author of 'The Sybarite', for it is clearly the
sequel to that story and so would reveal him as a boy-lover. But
Mackay, for his own purposes, was determined to keep his identity as Sagitta secret. The mystery still remained however: What
had become of the German original, and why was there an English
translation?

I have no answer to this mystery. Nor can I prove that Mackay
actually wrote this story. The internal evidence is there, but
without the German original we cannot even compare it with
Mackay's unmistakable style. If genuine, it furnishes an interesting insight into his psychology — both as an anarchist and as a
lover of boys. But even if the story is not by Mackay, that is no
reason to suppress it, for the following tale, presented here just as
I received it from the unknown Berliner, has a charm all its own.

V

Following that quite extraordinary evening spent with Germann, I could not get him out of my mind. For weeks I
would find myself thinking, 'the Sybarite would enjoy this',
or 'the Sybarite would avoid that'. In all that time, however,
I never once thought of Astruc cadet, even though Germann
had mentioned him a couple of times that evening and even

predicted that I would meet him again soon. Why indeed should I recall him? Our introduction by Germann in the Taverne Anglaise in Geneva had been much too brief. Thus Astruc was the person farthest from my mind when I stopped in Nice a month or two later. But it was there that I had my next encounter with him, an encounter that was to keep 'life's little loafer' uppermost in my mind for a long time.

Our meeting took place in a small Italian restaurant on the Promenade des Anglais. I was enjoying a delicious dish of *risotto alla milanese* and thinking what pleasure Germann would have taken in it, when Astruc, whom I did not immediately recognize, approached. 'Monsieur,' he said, speaking French, 'I'm delighted to see you again. Do you remember me?'

I looked up, annoyed that my dinner was disturbed, but even before I recognized him I was already under his spell. For a smile had spread across his face, the most charming I had ever seen, and all annoyance melted in its warmth. 'Astruc,' he said, holding out his hand, 'Astruc cadet. Monsieur Germann introduced us.' I immediately recalled him: Sybarite of Freedom, a Complete Anarchist — thus Germann had named him. I wanted to know why, and I asked him to join me. 'Gladly,' he said, and added as he sat down, ' Did Germann tell you I would find you again?'

Startled, for Germann had indeed promised just that, I mumbled some kind of reply, lapsing into German in my confusion, but Astruc continued, as though I had merely nodded. This habit of the French, of pretending not to hear anything spoken in another language, usually annoys me, but in Astruc's case it was only part of his charm. I doubt that he was able to speak a word that was not French — it probably never occurred to him that it might be necessary, for indeed he had no need. Not with me at any rate, for I have spoken French ever since my childhood travels in the South with my mother.

I was even more eager to talk with him now, for I was burning with curiosity to know why our meeting had seemed so inevitable to Germann and whether it was by chance, as it appeared, or if Astruc had somehow followed me from Geneva. As if to answer my questions immediately, Astruc said: 'Our friend Germann told me you were coming to Nice. He said he had detected a certain something about you that I would want to uncover for myself.' And he added, almost triumphantly, 'I think he was right!'

Far from satisfying my curiosity, Astruc's answer only added to the mystery. Still under the spell of his first smile, I thrilled at the suggestion of intrigue implied in his words. How little I anticipated the adventure that lay immediately before me and which was to remain one of my most beautiful memories! For the moment, however, he turned to other matters. He had not yet eaten; so, having inquired about my risotto, he ordered a plate just like it. But after glancing at the rather ordinary red wine I was drinking, he ordered an exquisite French wine from the waiter, adding, to me: 'You will allow me that, will you not, monsieur?' Oh Astruc, can one deny you nothing?

'What an invasion of my freedom!' I thought, however, and knew that I should have stormed at such an affront. Yet, in the next moment I found the most implausible excuses for his action and how gladly, yes gladly, I would pay for his meal. After all, I could easily afford it, and was it not worth it to see his enjoyment? If, as Germann had said, he was a Complete Anarchist, here was a new kind of anarchy. I eagerly began to question him about it.

'Not so fast,' he said, reminding me of Germann's words. 'Don't disturb the enjoyment of this meal. Later, while we linger over coffee and brandy, we can leisurely discuss the

topic. I know just the place — one you can easily afford,'
he added with a roguish twinkle in his eye. Ah Astruc, you
rascal, how you read my mind! But I laughed aloud, and he
joined in the laughter.

During the remainder of the meal we spoke only of
minor things: of the good weather Nice was enjoying and
of how delightful the sea was. 'And do you swim every day,
like Germann?' I asked.

'Just like him. It was he who taught me to enjoy it.' He
was silent a moment, then smiled as if recalling a pleasant
experience. 'I was only fourteen at the time we met. How
long ago that was!' (Long ago? He could not be more than
seventeen now!) Then, looking at me, he continued: 'We
met not far from here, but on an isolated beach. I had been
in the water already and was enjoying the solitude, but was
still a bit lonely. So I was glad to see the pleasant-looking
gentleman walking from the forest down to the beach. He
came right up to me and without any introduction
remarked: 'How much more you would enjoy your swim,
if you would strip off your trunks and allow the water to
flow evenly over your body. And how much more I would
enjoy watching you!' 'What a dirty old man!' I thought. 'But
why not? Give the gentleman a thrill. Oh I was a cheeky
kid!' (Was? And he now tells the story and hardly knows
me!)

'I stripped off my swimsuit then and there, and held it
out to Germann, asking him to hold it so that no thief would
take it while I was swimming, and ran back into the water.
He was right, of course; it is much more pleasurable to swim
naked. Naturally I was more aware at first of the sensation
in my exposed genitals, and I was quickly excited. A fourteen year-old is easily excited,' he added, and smiled with
pleasure after taking a long taste of his wine. Whether the
smile — and the reddish tint I detected in his cheeks —

came from recalling that excitement or simply from the alcohol in the wine, I did not know.

While Astruc was telling this story I had finished my meal and leaned back in my chair. But I found myself leaning forward again, hanging on every word. How frank he was! 'And did Germann enjoy watching you?' I could not resist asking.

'You bet! And when I came out of the water, he never took his eyes from me. I told you I was a cheeky kid. I walked right up to him, and he reached out and touched me. You know, there.' This time I turned red, and I looked around embarrassed, to see if anyone was listening. But even though Astruc had related all this in an ordinary tone of voice, it appeared that no one but I had heard it. The other diners were all absorbed in their meals or their own companions or both. Nevertheless, I was anxious to change the subject. So, remarking that we had both finished our meals, I suggested that we go on to the other place he had mentioned for our coffee and brandy, and I called to the waiter and paid.

Outside, we strolled along the Promenade. It was a warm, moonlit night and we could see the waves leisurely rolling toward the beach. Astruc, apparently having forgotten that he had related only the beginning of his meeting with Germann, was silent. I decided to change the subject and satisfy a curiosity. 'Did you know,' I asked, 'that Germann calls you a Complete Anarchist?'

'Oh yes. And he must be right — he usually is — though I am not sure I understand the term. But he told me that you have written a whole book about anarchists. Do you really know all about them?'

'Enough. But you have not read my book, then?'

'No. Germann has, and he told me about it.'

I wondered if Germann had also told him that my books

are 'sad', as he had remarked to me. But I asked, 'What is it you understand by the term "anarchist"?'

'Well, Germann explained that it comes from the Greek and means someone who rejects authority, that is, someone who doesn't let other people tell him what to do. And that's me!' And here he flashed again that charming smile.

'But do you want to tell other people what to do?'

'Why should I? It doesn't matter to me what they do, as long as they don't mess with me.'

'Did you always feel this way?'

'No. For a long time I was just a dumb kid. I thought, when I grow up I'll boss kids around the way people did me.'

'When did you change your views?'

'When I met Germann. He is an anarchist — and a quite extraordinary man.'

I knew that already. But I continued to question him. 'And did he not tell you what to do, when he told you to swim without your trunks?'

'But he did not tell me to do it. He only said that I would enjoy my swim more if I did. I decided. And like I said, I did it — and I was glad I did. We had a lot of fun together,' he added, and again there was that smile of pleasant recollection on his face.

But I could not let him get away with so easy an answer. 'So you admit that he talked you into it? That he used his authority as an adult or whatever to persuade you to do what he wished?'

'Well, yes, I suppose he did. But if he hadn't suggested it, I might not have tried it. And I did enjoy it!' For a moment he was satisfied with his answer, but then he added, 'You mean, suppose I hadn't enjoyed it — what then?'

'Yes, precisely.'

'I see. But how can you know if you don't try? And

anyway, what would the harm be? It wouldn't have hurt me. And Germann would have had his pleasure at any rate — for he did enjoy watching me.' And his eyes twinkled again.

'So he was right in asking you to do something for his pleasure, even though you might not enjoy it?'

'Yes. I mean no. I mean,' and he looked a bit irritated. 'You make everything so complicated. Who has time to think out all those things? Of course he wanted me to. He knew he would enjoy it; he was just as sure I would too. And he was right, wasn't he? You don't think Monsieur Germann would want to hurt me, do you?' he asked, almost with astonishment in his voice.

'No, of course I don't. But suppose it had been someone else?'

'Well then, I might not have done it.' And he looked a bit sad at the thought. But then he said with evident satisfaction, 'I'm glad it was Germann. He showed me how to do a lot of things.'

Naturally I was curious to know what those things were, but Astruc interrupted himself to suggest that we enter the little bar we were just then passing. 'Here is the place I mentioned earlier. I'm ready for coffee now. Aren't you?' I agreed to his suggestion and we entered. I needed no coaxing, for I was completely under his spell. How I liked this 'cheeky kid'!

We found a table in a quiet corner and I let him order for both of us the coffee and brandy he recommended. While Astruc was speaking to the waiter, I looked around the bar, it was not well lit, but after my eyes had adjusted to the dim light I was surprised to see that it was nearly full. I had been fooled by the quiet, for everyone seemed to be speaking in low tones. And not only low in volume, but also low in pitch. It took me a few moments to grasp the reason for this: there were no women in the place. I relaxed, for I often find high-pitched female laughter grating on my nerves. And then I tensed again. The men were speaking to one another softly and intimately. It was one of those bars! Would they think that Astruc and I were just another pair of lovers? Or would they be concerned because he was so much younger than I? I looked around to see if there were other couples where one was younger than the other and, seeing several, I relaxed again. Then I wondered if Astruc had chosen this bar for that very reason.

Astruc, having finished speaking to the waiter, again read my thoughts: 'I discovered this place only a couple of days ago and I immediately thought I should bring you here — if I saw you again.' This last was said, however, as if he had no doubt that he would. Oh Astruc, did Germann also teach you to scheme? By now, however, I was willing to let come what may. But I could not get over my scruples and I questioned my motives. Like Germann, I too would very much enjoy seeing Astruc swim in the nude. But would it be right to ask him to do it, as Germann did? Still, Astruc had completely justified Germann, and I suppose he would me too. But suppose it wasn't Astruc, but some other boy?

In this way, I tortured myself looking for some general rule. What worked in the case of Astruc might not work with another, but who that 'other' was remained vague, and so I had no answer. My thoughts stopped. It was then that I realized that Astruc was looking at me intently.

'Monsieur!' he exclaimed. 'I am here. Give me your full attention!' He said it sternly and I was a bit startled. Then we both burst out laughing simultaneously. And I laughed again because his laugh was so infectious.

We spoke of many things and, although I no longer quizzed him, I learned much about his background that interested me. His parents had neglected him, but an uncle had looked out for him and he had attended school long enough to learn to read and write. This uncle had died shortly after the meeting with Germann. Germann had taken him in for a while, but did not want to be tied down. Astruc would have liked to stay with him, but had also already learned that he could live on his own. He did odd jobs and he sometimes went with gentlemen, whom he met in bars like this one. 'But only if I liked them. And I made them pay.' He said it with a certain firmness, but added equally firmly, 'They got their money's worth!'

In the nearly three years since the meeting with Germann he had wandered a great deal, mostly along the southern coast of France. Once he had gone into Italy as far as Genoa on the coast and then as far north as Turin. He thought the Italians spoke French in a 'funny way', but a mathematics professor he met in Turin, who had been very nice to him, buying him an ice-cream and then taking him to a movie, had spoken very good French. He had been forced to return to France because the police kept asking him for his papers. He had no papers. 'Why should I carry "papers"?' he asked. I know who I am, and they have only to look at me. What did I do to them? Nothing. Why should they bother me?' And he looked at me as if I might have an answer. But he did not wait to see if I would answer him, and only added: 'The French police are not much better. Only they speak better French.' He smiled, as if this were some excuse for their actions. I suspected that it allowed him to better use his charms on them. I would have been surprised to learn that the French police had ever put him in jail. In fact, Astruc ended his tale with: 'They mostly just talked to me and let me go. Once a tall and very good-looking policeman took me home with him. That was a night!'

I saw my opportunity and took it. 'I have only a hotel room, but I would like to take you there with me. Will you spend the evening with me?'

'I thought you would never ask!'

The waiter gave Astruc a knowing look as we left, but I did not care. I was proud to be one of his 'gentlemen' and grateful that Astruc had found me that evening, though I was still unsure if it had been by chance or design. I could hardly repress my excitement as we walked to my hotel. I was breathing rapidly, in shallow breaths. But Astruc, although lively, had a calming effect on me. He made everything we did seem natural.

The concierge did not look up as he handed me my room key. When we arrived, I opened the door and let Astruc enter first. As I expected, he made a rapid survey of the room and then made himself comfortably at home. He seemed to become a part of the room — and its best part. No wonder the room had seemed so bare before, and how full of life it seemed now! In my discussion earlier I had learned that Astruc was indeed a Complete Anarchist. I was now eager to know what Germann had meant when he also called him a Sybarite of Freedom.

I opened a box of cigars. My plan was to enjoy a smoke while gently quizzing him in the matter. But Astruc had other ideas. 'Oh monsieur, please do not smoke! Not now at any rate. I only enjoy cigar smoke at a distance — and right now I want you to hold me close. You do want to, don't you?'

Could there be any doubt? I opened my arms wide. He came to me and fitted into them as if they were made to hold him, and indeed I felt at that moment they were. How comfortable I felt with him, and how I needed the feeling of his small body close to mine! Then a nagging doubt came back to me: was the pleasure his too? Or had I selfishly enticed him to my room? How can I repay him? I thought of his 'gentlemen' and somehow the arrangement seemed sordid to me. And yet, and yet ...

Astruc had no such doubts. But he did have an uncanny ability to read my thoughts. He made no effort to talk me out of my doubts; he merely snuggled closer and spread his arms around me too. Of course he wanted to be with me! As my doubts slipped away and I slowly relaxed in his arms, Astruc finally spoke: 'That's better. You are with me now, monsieur. Everything is as it should be. We are free to enjoy ourselves and each other. And I mean to enjoy you!' He raised his head and kissed me on the lips, twice — lightly at first and then warmly and firmly.

Suddenly overcome with emotion, I slumped onto the chair, while Astruc slipped between my legs. I again wrapped my arms around him, and now it was I who snuggled onto his breast. He put his hands gently behind my head and held me close. How protected I felt. The world seemed far away, or rather, all the world I cared about was with me now and in my arms. I wanted to protect this slim body that seemed to me so vulnerable. And yet it was he who protected me! Wanting to get even closer to this body, I unbuttoned his shirt and pressed my face against his smooth skin. As I did so, his hands held me tighter. Well-being flowed from that slender body into mine. I raised my head, kissed his neck, took his hands from behind my head, and kissed their palms, first the left hand, then the right. He then placed them against my cheeks, lowered his head, and kissed me full on the lips. 'Are you glad I found you again, monsieur?'

What could I answer? I wrapped my arms around his waist again and drew him close. Then I stood, lifted him up — how light he was! — and carried him to the bed. There I set him down, sat beside him, and wordlessly — I could not have spoken a word at that moment — took his shirt off him. The sight of that beautiful body brought the blood rushing to my face. His shoulders were slim, the muscles were just beginning to show in his arms, and when he lifted them and placed them around my neck, I caught a glimpse of the fine hairs just beginning to sprout under his arms. I wanted to keep my eyes wide open and drink everything in and at the same time I could not resist the urge to bury my face in the hollow of an arm. He allowed me neither, for his arms encircled my neck and with unexpected strength he drew my face tight against his. I knew in that moment that it was exactly what I wanted. Never, never has anyone ever anticipated my desires, my needs, as Astruc did that night!

'But you must undress, too, monsieur.' And without waiting for my agreement — what need was there? — he proceeded to unbutton and remove my shirt. He ran his hands through the hair on my chest, measured the width of my shoulders, and snuggled close. I ran my hands up and down his back. How smooth the skin was! How sweet the smell it gave off! Is there anything more wonderful in the world than the sensation of holding, possessing, a young and beautiful person like this?

It was a moment of sheer perfection. And then — how do such things happen? — a feeling, almost of remorse, came over me. My hands froze while my thoughts dashed madly. Have I a right to this sensation, this pleasure, this body? Do I deserve this happiness? Am I taking advantage of him? Shouldn't I think of him and his needs? And a hundred other such doubts suddenly rushed through my mind.

Again Astruc rescued me, and in his own simple, direct way. Again he read my thoughts. 'It is I who want you, monsieur. And I want you to touch me, there, where Germann did that first day on the beach.' The sly smile returned to his face as he said, in the same words he had used earlier: 'I am here. Give me your full attention!' Ah Astruc, how gladly I gave you my full attention! My fears again melted, as we both laughed at his impudence.

He immediately got off the bed, unbuckled his belt, unbuttoned his trousers, and stepped out of them, letting his underwear fall at the same time. He stood still a moment, while I gazed at his charming figure. He was slim, with small but tight muscles that appeared to be just on the verge of becoming large and manly. His narrow hips were firmly supported by unexpectedly shapely legs. His body hair was slight and very light in colour; it appeared to be bleached by the sun. Even the small amount of pubic hair was the same colour as the top of his head. The few freckles only served to call attention to the perfection of his skin. I could not get my fill of looking at this marvel. He could never have served, however, as model for an artist, for his beauty could not be captured on canvas or in marble. He was a living boy, on the verge of becoming a man, and that was something that no artist has ever fully captured, though many have tried. I willed the moment to last, but it was he who again broke the spell.

'Now you must undress, too, and I will enjoy looking at you.' But he did not wait for me to do so. As I stood to undress completely, he climbed onto the bed and lay on his back, his head propped onto the hands behind it. Nor did he look at me, but seemed to close his eyes. I undressed hastily, stepped back to the bed, and lay beside him. He turned to me, with eyes wide open, and said: 'And now let us make love. You do love me, don't you?'

Astruc, Astruc! Never did a question less need answering, and yet I answered it with all my being. Nor did I need to ask if he loved me. Our love making was inspired by an eros implanted in human nature, and we made no effort to restrain our passion. For minutes, one hour, two, we lost ourselves in a frenzy. I no longer knew where I was; I no longer cared to know. I only knew that Astruc had given me the freedom to love him in whatever way I wished, to love him my way. With no demands, no pressures, no limits, my pleasure was exquisite and boundless. But my greatest pleasure was to look at him, smell him, taste him, touch him — not just 'there' but everywhere — and to experience how my pleasure brou-ght his excitement to the height of ecstasy and beyond. All this was played through more than once, until finally Astruc, his energy spent and thoroughly satisfied, fell asleep on his pillow, contentment on his face.

I, however, could not sleep. Although the moon had long since set, the light of the street lamp came in through the window, which had been left open because of the warm night. The sleeping figure could be clearly seen, and lying beside him, propped on one elbow, I looked at the boy I loved and thought over the experience just past. Surely there were other boys in the world as handsome as he. Some of them were probably just as generous. What was it that made this experience so different? What was it about Astruc that was special?

I did not have to think long. It was our friend Germann who had given me the clue, though I did not know it at the time. He had called Astruc a Sybarite of Freedom. A Sybarite, surely — do we not all instinctively love pleasure? — but also a Sybarite of Freedom. With Astruc I had found at last the freedom to love, to love in my own way. And not just the freedom to love him, but others as well, for I felt now that I had been released from a bond I did not even know existed. The sense of freedom was overwhelming and my gratitude poured out to Astruc even as he slept. Oh Astruc, what can I do to show you my gratitude?

With this thought, a feeling of exhausted relaxation came over me and I lay back onto the pillow. As I did so, Astruc turned on his side and, in his sleep, laid his arm across my breast. Gently I placed my hand over his, and with my own smile of contentment, I too fell asleep...

I awoke the next morning with a sense of well-being, a feeling of being alive in a way I had never felt before. It took only a moment for me to recall the cause and turn to the source of my happiness. But Astruc was no longer there. Had he awakened early? Gone out for a coffee or a swim? It did not occur to me that I would not see him again that day, or ever again. I was nearly dressed when I saw the note, written in a rather childish hand, on the table. I have it yet, for I have guarded it like a sacred treasure. In his farewell Astruc wrote:

> My dear friend, I cannot wake you. You look so happy. But you would try to keep me, and I must go. I'm glad I found you again and I think you are too. Forgive me for taking twenty francs from your wallet. I need them for the next few days. Adieu, my dear friend. Remember me. Love, Astruc.

I have just copied out this note, but I know it by heart. I read it over and over. I was overcome by my loss: just when I thought I had found my 'friend for life', he had vanished. I knew immediately that any search was useless and I sat on the bed, on the edge of despair. What was I to do?

It was then that Astruc came to my rescue a final time, but in a way different from before. In seeking to recall what I had lost, I remembered what he had given me and I realized that it was something I would have forever: the freedom to love. Astruc had let me be free with him and I had learned to be free with myself. If I would never love Astruc again in the way I loved him that night, I knew that I could now love other boys in the same way. The sense of freedom again flooded over me, and again my gratitude poured out to Astruc, no longer there beside me on the bed. I still felt the loss, but I regretted nothing. And I knew that Astruc was happy, that I had made him happy. I had given him pleasure and he had taken pleasure. And that was as it should be.

I looked at the note again and one sentence stood out: 'But you would try to keep me, and I must go.' He was right: I would have tried to keep him. But with this thought he left me a final gift, for he also taught me not to try to keep a love that follows its own nature in leaving. I have since had to let go many times and it does not become easier, but always I think of Astruc and I know that I can. If Astruc did not understand the term 'anarchist' and would have laughed at being called a Sybarite, would he, I often wondered, have accepted the description I found for him? For I now understand and accept his right to be 'life's little loafer'.

Travelling

SUZANNE DANCE

For my mother, my grandmothers, and all the others, who 'provide the ground we walk on'. 'We are all of us paid for' keeps me going. An inspiration. This is the story of a daughter and her mother.

1954-56

SHE HAD prickly heat that summer. Her skin was pink and sore and itchy. She was four years old. The sticky heat of Singapore clung to her skin.

On the boat over she didn't eat. Her mother wondered. She went back herself. Back in time. A small house in England. She sat on the dark stair, afraid and angry.

Her Dad threw her make-up bag in the fire. He remembered his Dad thumping up the stairs to belt him.

So the Empress of China lives on. Layer upon layer of suffering and joy, like fertilizer to our searching.

What else could they do. Yearning and reaching and travelling grainy paths.

In the spring she began to feel better. She made friends. Went to nursery. Drank orange juice. Her brother was born in August. She watched his pink face, blond hair, small limbs. A prick. Her little brother. Now she loves him, but it took a while.

1920

Easton-on-the-Hill is a small village where her mother was

born. Honey-coloured stone among the green fields. Soft with age. In the left-hand corner of the White Hart pub. To Sarah, her Grandmother Daughter of Fanny Dance, a big woman. Strong and well-known in that village. Kept pigs, ran a pub, helped at births and deaths. A character. Fanny Dance. She took her great-grandmothers' name many years later. Her Dad wondered. She wondered. When did the story start. Whose shoulders bore the first burden. Whose joy shaped the first laugh. A great circle of lives — within a circle of life, a cycle, a great wheel, inside a wheel.

Urania

MAUD SULTER

'Les trois sur le trottoir le regarde passer
et n'y comprennent rien.'

COMPARED TO the composition of the Stars a photograph is no big deal. Any fix-ation of evidence or provi-dence or the like is but nothing compared to the fact that we can take flight through the heavens and visit each other just when we like. Isis she's got a big name for it down on earth and Nut well her reputation aint too bad either.

My sistah, she's pretty, in a plain sort of way, and I love her. She takes off with no prior warning and soars across planes of experience to come up with the most audacious ideas, and expectations. It sometimes takes the rest of us a bit of time to catch up with her but invariably we do and just as we get ourselves comfortably seated at the calabash off she goes on another flight of fancy so if that is the case we just pat each others arms and say, *'Girl what can you do!'* And then we eat the food, tell a few tales, drink some palm wine. If by the morning she hasn't returned we share a libation and wishing her all good vibes we get back to work; as cleaners, as doctors, as shop assistants, as scien-tists, as the like. Someday, maybe in a few days, sometimes it takes years, she'll just walk back in that door as though she'd just left to catch the last bus the night before. She'll kick off her shoes, she always wears real expensive ones says it's cause her feet are big and she can't get cheap ones that are comfy — let me tell you though — I know it runs in the family. She's got these photos of her Grandmother on her father's side and I can tell you something for nothing, that woman might have been walking on gold the price she must have paid for them sandals in those pictures — in any case in she'll walk back in without a by-your-leave. How's so and so she might ask, fine I might say and thingmy? Well thingmy passed on but you know who is still with us? Still with us after all these years she'll exclaim. And is there some groundnut stew? Sure I'll say and jollof rice and then I'll remember that she doesn't even come from the West coast but none the less she has a taste for these things says it runs in her bones.

Sometime later after we've got to know each other again she'll go to small marquesite chest and take out a locket. Then she'll kiss me gently and ask me to fix the clasp for her. And, I should know better, but I always ask, so how come you went away without it last time. Oh she'll say, like the time before. Well you know how it is. A locket with a picture is just that a locket with a picture. I sure like this locket with your picture. But when you're not with me I don't need it to remind me of you. I only need it when we're together so that I can remember to remember how you are when I'm with you to remind me of you when we're apart. Nothing on a fixed plane could remind me of you my woman of the universe. My love.

(Reproduced courtesy of Urban Fox Press.)

For The Love of Atalanta

MAUD SULTER

The voice of Atalanta
is like a celestial
choir.

The skin around the eyes
of Atalanta is almost
transparent so that
her eyes float, dark
islands, in honeytoned
pools.

The eyes of Atalanta
are thus veiled.

Ours is a mixed marriage
blessed by no Church. We
name our own saints and
ayatollahs. Sinners are
numerous in this House.

The narrowing of the Gulf
between us signifies
small victories. Almost
unremarkable however
remarkable still.

I.

I long to walk in forests
of pine on the West coast
of Scotland. The scent
clinging to the back of
the throat.

She longs to dip her gnarled
toes in warm pools of liquid
light on a Comoran
off the East coast
of Africa.

Then again, she adores the buzz
of the City while I droop
at the thought of
Kumasi marketlife,
sometimes.

Colours are our stock in trade
and there our tastes differ too,
for I am a child of the dark
imagination and Atalanta
a woman of the stars.

II.

Ours is a mixed marriage
blessed by no church. Our
religion is one full of self-
proclaimed communicants whose
blackness and womanhood are mantles
and their bodies altars unto which
we bring our prayers and saphies
to be sanctified.

We who will never be born again

are fortunate to recognise the wisdom
of the Elders who implored us to listen
to the heart and mind and not prostitute
ourselves in front of false Gods whose
only sacrament is the destruction of all
that is good and pure and true. In the name
of a fallen prophet. Doom-laden the vestments.
Caked with the bile of crusades. A Holy War
should be a contradiction in terms. But no.

III.
Our blood is red
Our love is woven
like an Ottoman rug
There is nothing
simple.

IV.
This marriage was made
in neither heaven nor
hell. It was born of
our blood which is red
nurtured in our flesh
which is black and will
be laid to rest at our
own hands. We hold the
key to its longevity
and do not shirk the
responsibility of its
death. For we who made
it live are warrior women,
gold blooded.

V.
Gold blooded warriors
convene in a zabat
each moontime.

Our Kirk
Our Temple
We shall overcome.

We shall overcome
not by endeavouring
to be more like them
in which ever guise
they come to peddle
their wares.

The myriad tapestry
of this life
is blessed by the
souls of the departed
who watch over us as we
track the continuum.

VI.
Ours is a mixed marriage
blessed by no church. For
this we thank the Goddess
Nut, may the stars arranged
around her head be forever
gentle, may the Sun to her
right hand and the Moon to
her left spin upon her fingertips
and may we as her supplicants
keep her spirit forever
with us. Our stigmata locks
as radiant as Sekhmet's.

For ours is a mixed marriage
which is as stable as our rock
of ages. Our foundations are
built on shifting sands which
sing. And with the voice of
Atalanta we drift and grow
to know our secrets.

The voice of Atalanta
The eyes of Atalanta
The mane of Atalanta
Let me sing of her beauty.

And I was let down amongst those people, without understanding their language or their ways, and I had to hide the fact that I was a stranger, and learn when laughter was appropriate, and when tears.

I made such an effort to reproduce their behaviour that I never actually decided what kindness was, or cruelty — the springhead of my feelings was blocked.

It was like interference coming on a television screen, and I'd have got up and twiddled the knobs, but I looked around me and realised that, for them, this was normality.

With that din in my ears, I discovered that they divided themselves into two sorts, women and men, and I was made like the latter, and when they told me

how I had to use my sex, I nearly burst out laughing. I stopped myself, but I thought — how could a woman and a man make someone? Don't they

... E fui calato in mezzo a quella gente

Christopher Whyte

Is chaidh mo leigeil sìos am measg nan daoin' ud
nach tuiginn an cainnt no 'n dòigh, is b' fheudar dhomh
ceiltinn gu robh mi nam choigreach, 's ionnsachadh
cuin' a bha gàire freagarrach, 's cuine caoidh.

Leis a leithid spàirn a bh'agam airson an gnàth
a mhac-shamlachadh, cha do shocraich mi gu fìor
dè bh'ann coibhneas, dè an-iochdmhorachd —
chaidh grab a chur air fuaran m' fhaireachdainn.

B'ann mar gun tigeadh buaireadh air sgàilean
telebhisein, 's bhithinn-sa ag èirigh
's a' tionndadh nan cnap, ach dh'amharc mi mun cuairt,
is thuig mi gu robh sin na riaghailteachd leò.

'S an sgreamhalachd ud nam chluasan-sa, nochd mi
gu robh iad gan roinneadh fhèin ann an dà ghnè,
boireannaich is fireannaich, 's mi dèant'
mar an darna cuid dhiubh, 's nuair a dhearbh iad dhomh

dè mar a chaidh mo bhall a chleachdadh, theab mi
gàireachdaich, ach bhac mi sin, is shaoil mi —
ciamar a bu chomasach boireannach is fear
air cuideigin a dhèanamh? Nach eil iad

*understand all that comes from somewhere else? It
seemed better to keep silent and pretend they were right.
But little by little, although my mimicry
was perfect,*

*their reality began to weigh on me, and I felt like crying
out that I didn't agree with all this. I scoured the faces I
came upon for a hint of irony
or scepticism —*

*but so that I wouldn't risk betraying myself — and, sure
enough, one day I could tell from the way a man was
looking at me that I wasn't alone.
But he got scared,*

*and ran away, leaving me with words rising to my lips
that I checked, and whose import I'd never find out. My
search grew more frantic after that*

*but it was useless. I'd have forgotten, have started
believing what they said around me, if it hadn't been for
music. My mother used to tell me how I spent an evening
in front of the radio,*

*transfixed, without moving, when I was still a child,
astonished at that miracle, because I knew it came from
there, and I was vindicated, justified! I often*

*thought I'd have done better to ignore that call, if I'd
been able. It was like being in a railway station, in a
crowd of people, swept*

tuigsinn gu bheil sin uile tàrmaichte
an àite eile? B' fheàrr leam gabhail gu clos
is leigeil orm gu robh iad ceart. Ach beag
is beag, ge foirfe 'n atharrais a dhèanainn,

thòisich an fhirinn ac' gam shàrachadh,
's bu mhiann leam glaodhaich nach deach mi le sin uile.
Sgrùdainn na h-aodannan a thachradh rium
airson sanas ioronais no às-creidimh —

ach air dòigh 's nach bithinn a' dol an cunnart
mi-fhìn a bhrathadh — agus, gu dearbh, aon latha
thuig mi bho mar a bha fear a' sealltainn orm
nach robh mi nam aonar. Ach bha eagal air,

is theich e, gam fhàgail le faclan a bha 'g èirigh
gum bhilean, is bhac mi iad, is cha do lorg mi
dè bha na bhrìgh dhiubh. Dh'fhàs an rannsachadh
a rinneadh leam na bu mhearanaich an dèidh sin,

ach bu dìomhain e. Bhithinn air dearmad,
air creidsinn na cluinnt' ga inns' mun cuairt orm,
mura b'e an ceòl. Bha mo mhàthair ag aithris dhomh
mar a stad mi fad an fheasgair ron rèidio,

air mo shàthadh, gun ghluasad, 's mi nam phàisdean fhathast,
air mo bhuaireadh leis a' mhìorbhail sin, oir thuig mi
gur ann bhon siud a bha e tighinn, 's mi
fireanaichte, ath-dhìolta! Nach ann

gu tric a smaoinich mi gun dèanainn-sa
na b' fheàrr nam b' urrainn dhomh an gairm ud
àicheadh. B'ann mar gu robh dòmhlachd sluaigh
mun cuairt orm, ann an stèisean, 's mi gam tharraing

*along with them, then seeing somebody I knew, far away
from me, hurrying in another direction, and I was filled
with longing for the place where we had been
together,*

*but I couldn't think where, and I stopped and shouted,
and tried to go after them, but the crowd was too strong
for me, and all I could do was stand and watch them
disappearing, leaving me there*

*without any idea what the bond that linked us was,
though it was so strong, and now the only hope I had of
finding out had just vanished. I discovered that music
could be written down,*

*and I went to the scores, and ransacked them, but all I
found was the footprints of people who could have
explained everything, and how can you live in a score?*

*Music was a place for me, or a signpost to a place, a
promise I would get there, a promise — even — of a
home. People who say your feelings get weaker*

*as you get older, and talk about clouds of glory, the
absolute purity of children, are wrong: the deeper I went
into music, the keener*

*my feelings got, as if something were rubbing against my
skin, and it got thinner and thinner, so that I couldn't tell
what was pain, what pleasure, and music became a
reason for tears.*

leò san t-sruth, is chithinn pearsa b' eòl dhomh,
ach fada bhuam, is cabhaig oirr', a' dol
an taobh eile, 's mi gam lìonadh le ionndrain
na ceàrna far an robh sinn ann le chèile,

's nach bu chuimhne leam, 's stadainn-sa, is dh'èighinn,
's mi feuchainn ri leantainn, ach an sluagh
ro neartmhor leam, 's cha b'urrainn dhomh ach stad,
is coimhead oirr' a' teicheadh, gam fhàgail ann,

gun fhaireachadh dè am bann, is e cho làidir,
a bha gar ceangal, 's an aon dòchas a bh'agam
air a nochdadh, direach air dol à sealladh.
Dh'ionnsaich mi gun deach an ceol a sgrìobhadh,

is chaidh mi chun nan sgòr, gan rannsachadh,
ach cha robh annt' ach lorg cas nam pearsa
a b'urrainn dhaibh gach rud a shoilleireachadh,
is ciamar a dheigheadh sgòran aiteachadh?

Is ann gu robh an ceòl na àite dhomh,
no sanas air àite, gealladh gu faighinn ris,
gealladh — eadhon — dhachaigh. Iadsan a chanas
gun tèid gach faireachdainn gu fàilneachadh

mar a dh'fhàsas duine aosd', a bhruidhneas mu
neulan na glòrmhorachd, mu fhìor-ghloin'
nam pàisdean, tha iad ceàrr: oir mar a chaidh mi
nas doimhn' a-steach dhan cheòl, is ann as gèire

dh'fhàsadh m' fhaireachdainn, mar gu robh rud
a' suathadh rim chraiceann, 's e sìor-dhol
an tainead, gus nach tuig mi de bh'ann tlachd,
de pian, 's an ceòl na adhbhar frasadh dheòir.

That was a sort of gradual remembering, as I put the pieces together bit by bit, each day more certain, more convinced, and growing calmer, for with the years I understood

that coming into the world is a kind of forgetting; that life is just a slow awakening, as reality encroaches on us more and more; and that death is only the gateway home.

B'e seòrsa cuimhneachadh neo-ghrad a bh'ann,
's mi cur nam piosan beag is beag ri chèile,
gach là nas dearbhta, nas cinntiche,
gam chiùineachadh, oir thuig mi bliadhn' seach bliadhn'

gur dìochuimhn' e a tha san teachd dhan t-saoghal,
nach eil a' bheatha ach na dùsgadh dàileach
('s an fhìrinneachd a' sìor-dhrùidheadh oirnn),
nach ann ach geata dhachaigh tha sa bhàs.

The Love That Dare Not

DAVID PARLANE

Even the illness that extinguishes it comes in borrowed
clothes, not one name but many, forming the syntax of
your end. Unravelling its hidden meanings, sidestepping
tears that dare not fall yet because they would admit the
last page of this dictionary has been turned, I trace you
back, nudging you, as I used to, from word to word:

the days you called me 'rinker', a tall, thin, long-legged
horse, a bloody harridan, I called you 'rintherout', a
gadabout, a needy, homeless vagrant, like the tongue we
spoke beneath the sheets. Our life as mobile and happy as
the half-a-dozen Scottish verbs I'd push across a page on
Sunday afternoons, trying to select a single meaning.

Here it is: under 'ripple' or 'rippill', a squat paragraph
which tells us we must separate the seed of flax from the
stalk, undo our badly-done work, separate and tear in
pieces. And when we are birds, must eat grains of
standing corn, when clouds, open up, disperse, clear off.
Its noun has you in its grip: an instrument with teeth for
rippling flax.

Or you might find us under 'set' which seats, places hens
on eggs in order to hatch them, assigns work, settles, gets
in order; puts milk into a pan for the cream to rise, sets
fishing-lines or nets, works according to a pattern, plants

potatoes, makes, impels, includes, besets, brings to a halt
and puzzles, nauseates, disgusts, marks game, lets, leases,
sends, dispatches, becomes, suits, beseems, sits, ceases to
grow, becomes mature, stiffens, congeals, starts, begins,
sets off

the love that dare not speak.   Except that now, so near
the end, when I would like to hold you and have been
forbidden, I search for it in your eyes, daring their
definition.

An Exile's Tale

BOB CANT

I OWE a lot to the *Dundee Courier*. Famed though it is for its front page advertisements, its neanderthal politics and its couthy news stories of Angus folk, the *Courier* was also the first publication to bring homosexuality to my attention. It was August 1957 and I was twelve years old. It was harvest time and far away in London the Wolfenden Report had just been produced. I have no way of knowing if any of my fellow harvesters were aware of its existence; it was certainly never discussed over the stooks. But for me it was the most rivetting news-story of my life; I read it and re-read it. I would like to go on to say that it was then that I acknowledged my own sexuality and began the struggle to be an openly gay man; it would not be true. What followed was much more complicated and took me a long way from D.C. Thomson's fiefdom.

I have no idea how I had learned about the existence of homosexuality before 1957; it had certainly not been as a result of experimentation. What shocked me about the *Courier* story more than anything else was that the word, the concept — homosexuality — was there in print for all to see. I remember being scolded for making jokes about fires and motor accidents on the grounds that the joke might make the real thing happen. The Wolfenden story somehow came into this same category of tempting fate. Would I become homosexual because I had read about the Wolfenden Report?

Wolfenden recommended that homosexual activity between consenting adult men over twenty-one in private
should be no longer a criminal offence. I could hardly
believe that there were men who were prepared to break the
law to have sex. In any country other than Presbyterian
Scotland this would have come as no surprise to an adoles-
cent boy, but in my isolated rural fastness this discovery was
on a par with learning about the discoveries of Einstein or
about the Russian Revolution. The whole world was turned
upside down. Sex outside the law of God was one thing, but
the fact that society would be prepared to consider condoning such godlessness completely undermined my understanding of what society was all about. And as for sex — I
did not even allow myself to think about that.

The next nine months are blocked from my conscious
memory. I had always been good at school but during this
period I fell back to nineteenth in my class. At the end of
this period I was resolved to become a minister in the
Church of Scotland. Girlfriends were not on my agenda.
Wanking and thinking about sex were thoroughly repressed
— all in the pursuit of Presbyterian virtue.

Friendship, of course, was acceptable and caring for
others became my speciality. Male and female alike, they
came to me with their woes and their pain and I, presumably
seeking Christ-like status, gave them nourishment. Well,
that was part of the story — the conscious part. But in the
autumn of 1959 I allowed myself to look at the muscular
thighs of the boy who sat next to me; and at his arms; and
at his back; and at the fold in his trousers. I was elated in
his company; we spent more and more time together. He
was everything I was not; good at football (hence the
thighs), cricket, golf; he was self-opinionated; a Tory; and,
worst of all, interested in girls. I offered him lots of nourishment but never dared to touch him. The State might be

thinking about condoning homosexual activity, but as for me — no chance.

I left my beloved sportsman behind when I went to university. It was only thirty miles away on the Fife coast, but it was so far away from the values of the *Dundee Courier* that I might as well have been on another planet. It was no longer taken for granted that you would fit somewhere into the Presbyterian framework. I enjoyed spending time with people of different backgrounds and different lifestyles and I found myself questioning Presbyterian values. The more I questioned them, the more I developed an independent identity.

Undergraduate life seemed very diverse to me and I learned a great deal about diversity of class and nationality. More problematic was the diversity of sexuality. Not only did I encounter heterosexuals who flouted marriage openly, but also people who were said to be 'queer'. They were said to be so on account of their use of the gestures and language that were, I came to learn, known as camp. Despite their charm and wit I was terrified by them. I could not understand how men could dare, so openly, to behave in a manner that would allow everyone to believe that they were homosexual. The fact that all the camp men I encountered were invariably English helped me to perceive homosexuality as foreign, as Other. To be both Scottish and queer must surely be an impossibility.

It was perhaps in search of such foreignness that I took myself off to the Edinburgh Festival at the age of twenty. Working as a dishwasher in an alternative theatre club, I revelled in being a tourist in such an exotic world. In no more than two weeks I had allowed myself to be lured into having sex with a handsome young Czech-American man. I can remember looking into the mirror the day afterwards to see if I had been changed by my first homosexual experience — I did not think about the *Dundee Courier* at all.

Holiday romances seldom last forever and when I
returned to university I did not consciously think about my
homosexual experience. Far from entering the world of
camp, I became much more confident on a number of
different levels. I joined the Labour Club and became a
member of the Student Representative Council. I became
involved with, first, one woman and then another, whom I
met through the Labour Club and I remain friendly with
both of them to this day. My homosexuality was not visible
to the world but it was no longer repressed. I went to the
room of another man to have sex on several occasions. We
never spoke during or immediately after the sex; we never
discussed its meaning on any other occasions. Eventually he
took to locking me out of his room. Twenty years later he
was able to tell me how much he had resented or admired
my ability to go for what I wanted, but at that time, I was
still utterly fearful about my homosexual activity and I
certainly never dared to speak its name.

My silence continued when I went to Tanzania. A one-
year teaching contract turned into two and a half years and
became one of the turning points of my life. I learned first
hand about the nature of imperialism and became fluent in
Swahili. My fluency enabled me to communicate easily with
the Tanzanian men I had sex with. There was no silence in
these relationships. But the language used within them was
not my own, permitting me, yet again, to distance myself
from my homosexuality.

This distancing process might have continued indefinite-
ly had I not gone to live in London in 1970. I was drawn
towards much of the revolutionary politics of the period
and began to commit myself to working for the creation of
a New World without exploitation or oppression or fear.
The most difficult part of that commitment was also to be
the one which was most personal and most long lasting: the

commitment to work for gay liberation. As well as working to support other people's struggles for control in their lives, I was also determined to work for a time in which homosexual people would be able to take control over their own lives — over our own lives. I was no longer prepared to distance myself from my homosexuality and I came out wherever I went.

The New World that so many of us strove for in the 70s and 80s changed its form, sometimes subtly, sometimes dramatically. For me there was one constant focal point — I remained openly gay and I worked to ensure that every campaign and organisation that I belonged to accepted the right of all lesbians and gays to be open and honest about their sexuality. Far from being isolated in this aim, I was very much part of a culture which shared these general assumptions. There were many differences within that culture and it was never static but that was where I belonged.

Thatcher's vindictive abolition of the Greater London Council in 1986 marked the end of one period in the history of that progressive gay culture. AIDS had already begun to make its mark on us all and whilst trying to face up to the issue of our own mortality we were also confronted by a new wave of bigotry. These bigots, who welcomed the deaths of gay men, blamed our whole community for the spread of HIV and used this epidemic as a justification for rolling back the few advances we had made for ourselves. Haringey, where I lived, became the site of a major ideological confrontation over the question of what children should be allowed to learn about homosexuality; homophobic bigotry was part of the Tory election atmosphere in 1987. One year later Section 28 of the Local Government Act banned the promotion of homosexuality in State schools.

It sometimes seemed to me that the only recourse was to protect and defend what we had already gained. The world we had created was stronger, more open and more diverse than the world of lesbians and gay men twenty years earlier but it was still far from the New World which we had hoped for; one free from exploitation, oppression and fear. The lesbian and gay community began to re-group, as it has always done, in the face of these new attacks. Some got into serious monogamy; some turned to the filofax culture; as for myself, I was no longer sure where I belonged.

It had not been part of the project of creating a New World for me to assert my Scottishness. As a teacher, I found that my accent caused disciplinary problems and I told myself that was why I lost much of it. Whilst I never pretended not to be Scottish, I never made an issue of anti-Scottish jokes in the way I did about anti-gay jokes. As I came to terms with my homosexuality I seemed to grow increasingly distant from my Scottishness. Although I was clear about the distance between myself and the world of the *Dundee Courier*, other dilemmas that I had about myself and Scotland remained unresolved. Scotland became the place I visited once or twice a year to see my elderly parents. One thing I knew for certain about Scotland was that I would never return to live there.

In the 1970s I read Lewis Grassic Gibbon's classic novel of Mearns farming folk, *A Scots Quair*. The farming community which Chris Guthrie came from was very similar to the one I had grown up in. At the end of the book, as both personal and political optimism vanish from Chris's life, she decides to return to live on her family's farm in the Mearns. The novel ends:

> Time she went home herself. But she still sat on as one by one the lights went out and the rain came beating the stones about her, and falling all that night while she still sat there, presently feeling no longer the touch of the rain or hearing the sounds of the lapwings going by.

To return home, as Chris Guthrie had done, seemed to me to be an act of despair, an act of resignation. An act which I was sure I would never make.

After the 1987 election when Labour increased its representation in Scotland a colleague at work remarked on how attractive returning to Scotland must seem to me. I explained, probably rather patronizingly, that it was not an option for me. I was well aware that the vote for Labour in Scotland was not so much a vote for socialism as a vote against the English nationalism of Thatcher. The Scottish Labour Party with only one woman MP in fifty and its apparent indifference to racism hardly seemed to be a place in which I would feel at home.

Later that summer I did return to Scotland for what was to prove to be a momentous visit. I decided to visit my family later than usual during harvest time. It had always been an important period in my life as a child and I wanted to see what had become of the corn fields that still haunted my memory. Thirty years before I had been part of the collective process of harvesting that corn. I knew that it was different but I had not faced up to the difference, in place of the corn was a particularly ugly oilseed rape. The groups of workers were replaced by isolated and stressed operators who drove their combine harvesters relentlessly from dawn to midnight. Rationally, it was foolish to be shocked by such technological change but shocked I was. A vision of my childhood had gone, and while it was traumatic it was also a relief. The *Dundee Courier* may have remained in a time warp, but now I was able to free myself from my Angus childhood.

In this emotionally raw condition I visited Glasgow on my way back to London; it was my first visit there in fifteen years. I found myself in an argument in the Waterloo Bar with a married gay plumber; the argument was about black

MPs. I was for them; he was against them. His arguments were what I imagined to be stereotypical of the Scots Labour Party; he saw mine as being stereotypical of the poseurs who were wrecking the London Labour Party. We had sex later in a wood near Easterhouse and I never saw him again. That might well have been the end of that, but there was something about the quality of our argument which struck a chord in me. Had I been in London any such argument would doubtless have been clever, sectarian and touched on nothing other than politics. This argument dug much deeper. Despite our differences, there was a common ground that we shared, a set of values, a set of assumptions, all of which arose from the fact that we were both Scottish. I felt as though a whole set of emotions about which I had been very defensive had been released.

This could have led to an adoption of national chauvinism on my part, an embracing of nostalgia, but instead it led me to Gramsci. In the Prison Notebooks he had written:

> The personality is strangely composite; it contains Stone Age elements and principles of a more advanced science, prejudices from all past phases of history at the local level and intuitions of a future philosophy which will be that of a human race united the world over ... The starting point of critical elaboration is the consciousness of what one really is and is 'knowing thyself' as a product of the historical process to date which has deposited in you an infinity of traces ...

Still the rationalistic optimist, I was drawn to this intellectual explanation for the very irrational process I was going through. I would never be able to reach or even articulate the New World of my dreams if I did not acknowledge the Old World from which I had come. The world of Angus farms, of Presbyterian self-righteousness, of belief in a common good, the world of the *Dundee Courier*. I did not have to endorse any of these 'traces' but I did have to acknowledge them as part of my history, as part of the process of learning more fully to know myself.

Over the next year I became more emotionally open to Scots influences. Previously my interests would have been largely limited to political events and while there were plenty of those in Scotland in 1988 I also became more alert to a wider range of Scots 'traces'. I found myself listening to progressive modern Scots music — Hue and Cry and Runrig. I discovered the Colourist school of Scots painters. And, not least in the scale of things, Scotsmen seemed to be more sexually desirable than ever before.

The acknowledgement of the Scots 'traces' led me to acknowledge and face up to other 'traces' and other feelings which I had kept hidden and repressed. It had long been part of my political belief system to accept the kaleidoscopic nature of human existence. Now I found myself able to accept more fully the kaleidoscopic nature of my own existence. I was particularly able to come to terms with experiences which I would once have seen as overly sentimental. I became, at last, able to enjoy opera — probably the second last gay man in Europe to do so.

A major turning point was a visit to see a play by Clyde Unity Theatre in which the central character was a man who was both gay and Scots. 'Killing Me Softly' is a powerfully emotional play and I wept through most of it. My tears were partly tears of amazement that such a play was being performed before such a friendly audience; they were also tears of celebration about the weight that was being lifted from me. I did not have to choose between being Scots and being gay.

The strong sense of belonging that I increasingly felt in Scotland did not mean that I had to adhere to every part of

Scots culture. I could, as I had done in 1957, read the *Dundee Courier* without having to accept all its values. It was September 1988: I was forty-three years old; and it was harvest time in Angus. But I was in Edinburgh and I knew that my emotional exile was at an end.

My physical exile began to come to an end in December 1989. I was being interviewed for a job in Edinburgh when I did something that I would never have imagined possible thirty years previously at the time of the Wolfenden Report or twenty years previously when I went to live in London. I openly declared myself to be gay. I was offered the job and moved to Edinburgh on my own terms in April, 1990 — but coming home is never the end of the story.

lullaby

JAMIE MCCALL

lie down and let
me divest you
of your rougher outer habits.

in particular i am
interested in tearing
at the straight seer of

your jeans, envied
day-long
as they shape blue

your crotch, moving
over is not
necessary: this ideal

bedding allows
me to fit my
form around

your gentle centre, sleep
as my imperfect
kisses and caresses permit.

a kiss that lingered

ALAN DAVID TAYLOR

a kiss that lingered long across my life
a hanging threat
unfolding slowly slick
the story of my life

connecting
all I was
to
all I wanted now to be
caressing quiet loves alive
to mad adept insanities

a kiss that lingered long across my life
a thread of comfort
tied around my heart
armlinking all
the good
to
baddest bads of me

placing high
the circling spirit of my soul

a kiss that lingered long across my life
a warming shadow
spent across
my breathless cares

hard shoving me
to
untold stories of delight

splitting wide
the darkest secrets of my chicken heart

Family Matter

FLORENCE HAMILTON

THE GROUP, LONDON, 1979

'I got married wanting my father. He was the only member of my family who came to the wedding, and he had been dead for just over a year. As we stood together, Michael on my right and Dad on my left, I could feel his discomfort in a stiff collar and tie as much as mine in high heels, clip-on earrings and a pale yellow dress labelled artificial silk.'

Nobody said anything. I decided to wait a while before moving on to my theory of contact through astral projection taking place around the time of death. I knew how disruptive certain members of the group would find it although I was obsessively sure of my ground.

The six of us met once a week to do feminist therapy. We had already survived a major conflict over theory and practice. For some it had been traumatic but for others it was just tedious. My position in the group shifted from off-beam outsider to unaligned excursionist, depending on one's point of view, and I would play willingly with its structure. Fortunately the group leaned towards organic development; one week we would set a rigorous agenda, the next would be an anarchic brainstorming session. I hoped V I Lenin never got to hear of it, although if he did it would prove everything is more complicated than we think. He came low on my list of desirable contacts but if the opportunity arose I thought I could teach him something about the lessons of history.

After the several minutes' silence, which everyone was supposed to use constructively in order to avoid the use of cliche in responding to the speaker, the atmosphere could become slightly oppressive. Sometimes it took over and we would sit speechless until someone asserted herself and, trying not to sound too apologetic or too flippant, suggested making a pot of tea. More often, the one who saw herself as a facilitator would sense the need for urgent action and make a remark that, although not skysplitting in originality, would take us thankfully forward. The facilitator took pleasure in separating fantasy from fact and understood the need to impose order on an unlikely story. With this in mind and unaware of the insult, she offered: 'Maybe Michael reminded you of your father?'

It was not a question of likeness, I said stiffly as if speaking an unfamiliar language. At least not between those two. Not for the first time, I wished I had insisted on the right to drink at these meetings. Like father, like daughter.

Father-Daughter Relationships in Group Work: what did your father give to you? (Not a popular workshop theme, mothers being much more in fashion at the time as part of the female cycle. It was possible to lose friends by criticising mothers.) A personality that took to drink, dominoes, depression and deviancy as if they were essential requirements for making progress in life. A chip on the shoulder, discarded but persistent and eventually welcomed, stroked and polished. Just like your father, she would accuse, I wash my hands of you. Two of a kind, I would say proudly, you haven't had much luck. I would have to work harder to like my mother if I was to become a good feminist.

A large round-faced clock was presented to my father to

commemorate forty-five years fitting parts of engines together in what had been the railway workshop of the world. Victorian England's housing conditions lasted longer in Glasgow. It was well into the 1960s before the railway works were closed and homes destroyed to make way for a post-industrial culture that would fail to impress the unconverted with its superficiality and its self-conscious, mannered performance. How could tenements be reconstructed in a museum? I stood on blowy street corners looking at the rubble of half-demolished buildings with gutted rooms hanging exposed and humiliated in the drizzle, wondering whose home would qualify for preservation.

BUTE, 1960

Early on, united by blood and divided by age more than anything, the two of us had an agreement to stick together. In the faded holiday snap I am eight, he is fifty-one. Hand in hand we walk past the Gallowgate Post Office, in step made perfect by Saturday afternoon practice which always ends in our favourite café with a celebratory ice-cream called McCallum. Dressed in identical navy-blue blazers bearing personal emblems on each breast pocket, we screw up our eyes against the unexpectedly fierce sun and pay a smiling street photographer. He dances pleased in front of us wearing a striped suit, because we are so keen to see the result of his work. We want to see ourselves together, to know that this is what matters.

Three years later gran died and I was sent to spend the summer holidays with Dad's sister in Ayrshire. I wasn't sure what mentally disturbed meant, but the plan was for me to go home when my mother had recovered. It was an act of mercy as far as these unknown relatives were concerned, and would be the last time they had anything to do with us.

'Shena'll see you all right', Dad said. 'Here's a fiver. I'll come and get you in six weeks.'

Shena made up for her mother's malice. She had been waiting for me, she said. She had looked out special clothes that were too small for her now but would be just right for me, she knew, she had seen the photograph Dad sent. We had a whole summer and there was a lot to do.

That night we sat on Shena's big bed with clean blue sheets and a purple-flowered quilt. By the window overlooking the allotments a tall, dusty mirror leaned on one foot, draped with coloured scarves and strings of poppets and glass beads. There was a high-backed chair cushioned in dark-green velveteen. I recognised the material. My mother had wanted velveteen curtains for the big room. In a dim corner the door of a heavy-shouldered double wardrobe hung open, pushed out by the jumble of clothes stacked inside. Piles of neatly folded dressmaking material lay on the floor. The room smelled of new cloth and the real vegetables growing outside.

Shena walked over to the window and drew the curtains so that we still had a bit of light. Fabric from the home furnishing department's better, she said, you get more variety, nice silky stuff that hangs well, you can do more with it. Mum keeps saving remnants for me, but I'm not interested in floral prints.

Pulling off her striped sloppy-joe, she dabbed 'Midnight in Paris' behind her ears and under her arms, and held out two lengths of material, one pale green with a white pattern and one dark red. 'The red, I like that best.'

Without her clothes she looked older, smooth and practised like a model in a magazine, but I didn't feel left out. I helped her make a costume and looked in the big wardrobe for a pair of brown leather sandals with thin straps, and she held out her narrow, sharply-arched feet so I could do them up. Shena's toes were just right for sucking and she never put on nail-varnish. Sometimes we stroked each other under the costumes in our private play, but she was never happy for long. We always had to think up new ways for Shena to show off her body. Not that I minded giving her so much attention.

Hand in hand the two of us walked down the drive away from Shena's house, Dad carrying a suitcase they'd given me with some of her clothes that she'd grown out of. I listened to the stories about my mother's nervous breakdown, gran's funeral, all the cousins emigrating to New Zealand in search of jobs and money, and thought about becoming Shena's pen-pal, writing clever, amusing letters full of imagination and daring words. Shena never wrote back to me. I always blamed her mother. And I blamed mine for what happened to Dad. Both of them would be lost to me for a long time. A man I met later said I would find answers to all my questions in the occult sciences. Psychical research had shown that contact could be made with proper training. By that time everything had changed.

GLASGOW, 1968

Billy's accident happened about two o'clock in the morning on a Wednesday, the night before I had my history 'O' level exam. I was already used to hearing the voices, louder as they staggered up from the pub on the corner, past the church and the butcher's shop. Their bodies fell heavily against the stone wall at the front close. Shouting to each other to be quiet, they would carry Dad up the stairs and drag him to the door where my mother would have been standing listening to the noise coming up the street. The dinner was always still hot as a matter of pride.

Usually I stayed out of it, but this time it went on for a long time. What upset me was Billy lying still on the floor, his metal cage with its stand knocked over on one side, the door bent back, water trickling out of the blue bath onto the matted orange rug by the electric fire. Seed had got scattered around and bits of cuttlefish floated in a cup of tea on the mantelpiece, like chunks of creamy ice in a bottle of milk that's frozen. Clutching his striped pyjama-jacket, my father lay naked and unconscious. I went back to bed and read about Roundheads and Cavaliers, revising until it was time to go to school. There was a question about the English Civil War, but I could remember nothing.

Seven years later at his cremation three Salvation Army bandsmen in uniform shook hands with everyone, old friends despite our failure and the trouble caused by the drink. They were concerned about my mother's state of mind, having lost her husband after years of strain and distress and without the comfort of her daughter who, although she had put in an appearance, was clearly no help at all and looked ready to leave. It was common knowledge that I had run off to London with no job and no friends or people to stay with. A big man with red veins on his face, looking as if he took more than an occasional drink himself, said that regular Sundays plus two nights' band practise had tired Dad out, and with chronic bronchitis it would have been madness to carry on playing.

LONDON, 1976

The day after I went for Michael with a bottle he asked our doctor to come and talk to me. This is about as much as I can take, he said. She's a woman, maybe you can tell *her* what's turning you into a raving loony. You're my *wife*, after all! Sitting on the floor in a corner of the living-room wrapped in a blanket, I thought it was strange to hear this from a soft-faced, self-styled hippy too sensitive to go out into the hard world of PAYE. From someone who preferred to jam into the early hours secure in the knowledge that his parents would rush to the rescue with cheques and food hampers should the need arise ... should his marriage to this clearly unsuitable girl who worked as a secretary and had been seen by Michael's sister kissing another woman in a crowded public place begin to show signs of falling apart.

Before going to sleep at night I read: 'The Astral Body may be defined as the Double, or the ethereal counterpart of the physical body, which it resembles and with which it normally coincides. It is thought to be composed of some semi-fluidic or subtle form of matter, invisible to the physical eye.'

It was difficult to convince the doctors, those young and attentive psychiatry students, and especially, later on, the sisters in the therapy group, that I had succeeded in absorbing Dad's spiritual body around the time of his death. For me the question was not to do with the possibility of it happening at all, but whether a counterpart of his physical body could in fact become part of my own. As far as I knew there was no record of this kind of male to female merging but anyone who knew our history — was it really only Shena who did? — would recognise it as a logical process.

Contacting Shena has not been so successful. Years of writing letters, going back to the house she lived in, asking neighbours if they knew where she might have gone, have all come up with nothing. I know what she did, though, and in a way it suited me quite well to hang around off-licences in front of stacks of Tennents lager cans looking at the models. Heather and Moira were very popular, and so was Shena. They were on most of the cans, then the pictures changed and I didn't recognise any of them.

So in answer to your question, it was not a matter of likeness between those two, my father dying undeserving of his sister's love, remembered as a railwayman but unrecognised as a musician, unable to find a quiet place to forget about an engine-fitter's life, to think about the lessons of history and how to beat the booze, and my husband, a privileged boy sitting in drug-induced peace writing songs with his friends. Dad, Shena and me. That's what mattered.

They're Playing the Trumpet —

CHRISTIAN MCEWEN

WHEN I say 'New York', I do not mean Brooklyn or the outer boroughs. I do not even mean the full length of the island of Manhattan. When I say 'New York', I mean what most folks now call 'the East Village' or 'the Lower East Side': a tiny piece of land, just over one mile square. It is a zany, painful, continually surprising place, which over the years has become (that wholly American reassurance) my neighborhood.

When I first came to Manhattan in 1977, I did not even visit that New York. I stayed on Broome Street with some friends of my uncle and gave myself up to being an obedient tourist. I remember the tall grimly-lit buildings the night I arrived, the taste of Dutch apple yoghurt at the breakfast table. I remember the green skirts of the Statue of Liberty, the piped music at the Cloisters, the pointed roofs of the water towers from the top of the Empire State. I visited the Modern and the Met., sent postcards home. I had no idea of what I was not seeing, how very much I was being taken care of.

Five and a half years later, I came back to New York to live. I had no job, no apartment, and knew a total of about six people. But my old lover Nina was following her new girlfriend to the city, and I thought if I was patient, then maybe I could win her back. I had finished my degree in

California, there was nothing there to keep me. I had just turned twenty-six. And in New York, why, anything could happen.

At first I planned to live on Staten Island. The ferry-ride, I thought, would be a pleasure every day, and Robert Lowell had had a house there, and at that time, Audre Lorde. The rents were cheaper too. I checked the *Voice*. But the day my search began, Deborah K., typesetter and apprentice clown, had put in an ad for a three-month sublet on Avenue B. I saw the ad. I called the number. And that evening, when I walked in the door of Deborah's apartment, and saw the great silver coil of her susaphone, her snake, Dr Henry Martin, asleep in his glass box, and the Kandinsky posters bright against the walls, I said immediately, 'This feels like home!' Deborah seemed to think so too. A couple of days later, I moved in.

I loved Deborah, her glossy black hair and her strange eyes: one blue-grey, and one parti-coloured, blue-grey / brown. She had a long tongue like a lizard's, and square thumbs, the shape and intensity of big toes. It was as if she'd known her destiny in the womb, and made sure she came provided with the appropriate props. We lived well together, efficient and companionable, sharing the chores, listening to each other's stories. The apartment was a joy. But the outside was another matter. The immediate neighborhood was one of the worst in the city.

Deborah's building was on Avenue B and First Street, opposite a well-known 'heroin hotel'. You could stand at the kitchen window and watch the junkies shooting up: a bizarre kind of puppet-show. At any time of day or night the air was filled with the noise of lackeys calling out their dealers' wares, and when you looked down into the street there were often as many as fifty people circling and prowling. 'Toi-let! Toi-let! Mr C — Cocaine! Blue Tips!

Red Devil! White Horse! Excalibur!' These strange phrases were the brandnames of different drugs, usually heroin, which at that time went for ten dollars a deck (enough for one shot). 'Fly with me, fool!' read the mural on East Sixth Street, a beautiful painted eagle dangling a syringe in his golden claws. It was entirely too apt. Junkies, muggers, and their hangers-on came from all over the five boroughs and beyond. Often, half asleep, I'd hear a scream or a cry of outrage, catch the tail end of a scuffle out of a window, see the flash of a pair or handcuffs or someone running, fast.

Listening to Deborah, asking questions, I began to get a grasp on what I saw. My journal of the time is tense with noticings, mind stretching to accommodate extraordinary new facts. *The fear of walking two blocks to the bank. The screams on the street. 'Works! Works!' The couple handcuffed on Houston. The kids throwing rocks at the street-lamps. The fire in the blue house opposite Deborah's, firemen like divers, all in padded black, with yellow hoses, swarming up a ladder.* From Turk, a part-time wheeler-dealer, I acquired more information: street slang, street-scenes, the price of dope, the different kinds of knives:

> *'Hollywood' means the police are coming, move. If you don't, you may get your throat cut afterwards.*

> *Butterfly knives: the only flick knives to be trusted. They open on both sides like a Japanese fan.*

> *$100 for a gram of coke. $15 for five or six lines.*

It was as if I felt such accuracy would protect me, teach me once and for all how life was lived on B and how to deal. But however many details I accumulated, I still was very often frightened. Leaving the house meant walking out into a screaming market-place. Dealers and junkies lounged against broken furniture and burnt-out cars, took over the sidewalks and the stoops of houses. Coming home again was just as bad. I learned to be firm and matter-of-fact approaching the front door, key tight in my fist. 'Excuse me, can you let me through please?' And then the sharp slam shut, so that no-one would push in behind me, the utter silence leaning up against the wall, belly slack, heart thumping with relief.

By New Year I had joined a self-defence class on Fourteenth Street. *Lots of kicks. I learned to kick backwards. Felt glad/sad to be in a class with children. Admired the conviction of their shouts. 'You're beating your last mugger,' said one woman to her son. Poor guy: fat, thirteen or so.* Over the weeks I learned to punch a sand-bag and to shout, to slash upwards with the side of my hand, catch the little bridge of membrane between the nostrils, bring tears to someone's eyes. I began to accept that it was *all right* to turn around and stare if I felt in any way uncomfortable, that frequently the best thing was to run. It seemed odd to know these things, to *expect* trouble. Growing up in Scotland, in the country, I had been trained above all to be 'nice'. And there were nice people on B too: families, local folks. It was just that you couldn't count on anything. *Last night when I came back from Ludlow Street there was a policeman opposite Deborah's house and nine men lined up with their faces to the wall. A lot of excitement among the Spanish-speaking women. 'That'll teach them.'* Once I watched an entire bust from the safety of the kitchen window: plainclothes policemen holding shot-guns; men in handcuffs, heads pressed down against the hoods of cars; wads of notes recovered, orange plastic syringes. I remember noticing painfully that all the cops were white, all the dealers black or Hispanic.

For myself, white and single, and (although I didn't know

it then) to some extent 'upwardly mobile', questions of race and class and their various ramifications were never far away. Although life on B was utterly astonishing to me (and to other people too — 'You *live* here?' asked a cab-driver late one night, looking round in horror at the devastation), it was not the only life that I had access to. There were days in silent libraries uptown, researching the Princess of Jansi (the Indian Joan of Arc) for my unlikely employer Prince Michael of Greece. There were days spent building bookcases downtown, days on the phone looking desperately for work, days remodelling a large apartment on Central Park West. In the course of that year I learned to put up sheetrock, to tape and mud and spackle and plaster; to use a screw-driver and a tape-measure and an industrial vacuum-cleaner; to stand on a shaky ladder and operate a screw-gun with one hand. If I did not succeed in winning Nina back, at least she was in my life as friend and workmate and companion. We had joined a writing group taught by Gloria Anzaldua. Some weekends we visited Kate Millett's Farm up near Poughkeepsie. And the city itself was a pleasure to explore.

Once out of B, I loved the immediate neighborhood: the beautiful lithe poplars in the empty lot on Houston; Essex Street with its cream cheese and lox and sturgeon stalls, its pickle barrels crammed with pickles like gigantic warty fish; Economy Candy with its biscuits and dried fruit, its velvety chocolate smell. I made a list of 'Things to be glad of in NYC' which included *the names of the subway stops: Bleecker, Astor and Spring; Kate's pink door; the short walks and the long ones; the busyness of snow*. More than anything I liked what Nina called 'going on a wander' down to the East River to watch the tugs and barges going by, off through Chinatown for soup in the Mayflower Cafe, and on to Bayard Street for delicious ices flavoured with mango or ginger or green tea. Often, after work, she and I would take off together, faces up, dazzled, to the cobbled sky, crazy-paving stones of cloud with light behind. I remember a snowstorm which brought the whole city to a blissful standstill, white on white like an enormous flowered tablecloth. And then the hubbub of spring, cherry trees alight in Central Park.

But always, for me, it was the people who mattered most. Not the dealers, not the junkies, but the ordinary neighbor-hood folk: *the tiny Hispanic child on Easter morning, all dressed up in lace and flowers, how she paused at the side of the (filthy) street), swinging her be-ribboned basket, how even her socks were edged with lace. The guy on B the other night, sitting on his ghetto-box and blowing bubbles out into the street. The black transvestite in his copper-coloured wig, sitting on the doorstep painting his/her finger-nails.* I wrote it down. I couldn't not write it. *A small boy on Allen Street, who decided to make friends with me, showed me a frog he'd bought at the pet-shop and was carrying home in a paper-bag. The fat woman leaning out of the window, resting her huge breasts on a comfortable cushion. The Pentecostals speaking in tongues (Span-ish) as my friend Roz and I walked by.* Letting one scene flare up in the memory and ignite another, I think of Whitman and his tremendous catalogues:

> The machinist rolls up his sleeve — the policeman travels his beat — the gate-keeper marks who pass.

> The groups of newly-come immigrants cover the wharf or levee.

> The prostitute draggles her shawl, her bonnet bobs on her tipsy and pimpled neck.   (*Song of Myself*, p.28)

I needed such a form myself: huge, inclusive, open-ended.

My one square mile of neighborhood was more than I knew what to do with. I felt that even then, hunched upstairs on weekends over my 'real' writing: poems and fairy-tales, remembered family stories. What was I after, sitting in the middle of the ghetto writing lesbian love-poems? What was this pastoral mush? The neighborhood was invariably more interesting. *They are playing the trumpet out there in the street. I must wipe my early morning fury from my eyes and see what can be done. The sun is shining.*

I do not know how long I would have lasted on Avenue B. As things turned out, it was less than a year. In the June of 1983 my brother killed himself. I went back for one funeral and stayed for another. In September of that year my sister Kate was drowned.

For the next couple of years I lived in London, reading manuscripts for the feminist press Virago, teaching creative writing in a couple of adult education institutes. I reconnected with old friends, made several new ones. People were kind to me. But still I missed New York: its exuberance, extravagance, its challenges and contradictions. I visited the States in the summer of 1984, and again in the spring and summer of 1985. In January 1986 I moved back there to live. By November I had found myself an over-priced sublet, two blocks south of Avenue B. It was dirty and run-down, with ugly pinkish-yellow walls, but the view flared out to the north-east, under a wide sky, and the rooms, once painted, looked fresh and bright and spacious.

In the three and a half years that I'd been gone, the Lower East Side had changed. Gentrification had taken over with a vengeance. There were shoebox-sized art-galleries in the numbered streets running east towards the river; Italianate cafés replaced the old bodegas. And, most noticeable of all, 'Operation Pressure Point' had cleaned up the old drug-market on Avenue B.

I went to the library and read about it in the newspaper: how it had started back in February of 1984: drug-vans lined up in Tompkins Square Park, police on horseback patrolling the neighborhood. They had brought in 150 regular cops, working two shifts a day for the duration. Within three months there had been 4,000 drug-related arrests. By the end of the year there were no street-dealers standing in the avenue crying their wares, no shambling junkies in from out of town. The drug-trade didn't disappear, of course. The local economy was too shaky for that. People needed the hundred bucks a day they could earn as lookouts and runners. But the dealing that remained was much more circumspect. The real estate people insisted upon that. They had co-ops to sell, customers to reassure. Prices were going up all the time. An empty rubble-strewn lot on East Sixth Street, with no building on it, nothing, was already valued at $250,000.

These of course, were yuppie figures, impossibly out of reach for local people. 'MUG A YUPPIE' read the graffiti on the wall of the supermarket. 'DOWN WITH YUPPIE SCUM'. The number of available housing-units had actually *decreased* in the neighborhood (as opposed to elsewhere in Manhattan), and most people had trouble even finding an apartment. The contrast with the newcomers was hard to bear. Even for someone like me, with all the privileges of skin colour and education, there was brutality in that thrust of riches: stretch limousines drawn up to the sidewalk, carrier bags from Balducci's or Dean & DeLuca. After years of shouting up to friends because their buzzers didn't work, swearing at the shower because the water had given out (again!) it was infuriating to know that right around the corner there were sleek smooth elevators leading up to enormous apartments where everything worked, where there was heat in winter and air-conditioning in summer, where the outlets provided electricity and the faucets didn't drip, where the roaches had long ago been eliminated. No wonder people were angry. The drug clean-up, of course, had largely been a matter of appearances. Other neighborhood problems remained completely untouched: street crime, illegal dumping, prostitution, sudden unexplained outbreaks of arson. Chief among them, and growing always worse, was the problem of homelessness.

In the fall of 1982, soon after I moved to New York, I was walking west on Houston Street across the Bowery. There, on the far side of the street was a huge freestanding wall, painted by Keith Haring in pink and black and fluorescent orange. In front of the wall stood an elegant uptown model in a green autumnal suit. Directly behind her, in the banked-up rubble on the other side, an old black man was taking a pee. I was so close I could practically hear his water as it hit the ground. But the model went on modelling. Her camera-man continued unperturbed. And even as I watched, the old black man pulled himself together, and went shuffling off about his business.

Looking back now, I remember the shock of that juxtaposition, not just the economic contrast or the racial one, but the fact that all parties took it absolutely for granted. *And how could it be otherwise?* they seemed to ask. *We live on an island thirteen and a half miles long by less than three miles wide. There are one and a half million of us. How else could we have privacy and focus in our lives?*

Since 1980, homelessness in New York City has gone up by 500%. There are homeless people everywhere you look.

I see them at night in the subway stations, row on row. They lie on cardboard boxes broken open to serve as mattresses, their few possessions huddled close to them, old coats and blankets thrown across their bodies. By day they stay near to the shelters and soup-kitchens, wiping windshields for a quarter on Bowery and Houston, panhandling on Second Avenue. In the newly gentrified neighborhood, their ragged presence stands out sharply. I was particularly struck by a beautiful yuppie restaurant on Broadway and East Third Street, its plate glass windows glittering in the afternoon sun. Blue balloons bobbed in the windows over menus offering such items as 'shrimp Veracruz', 'fried ice-cream' and 'kahlua mousse'. But on the side of the building, just above eye-level, someone had lettered in clear capitals, PEOPLE STARVE ON THIS BLOCK.

When I arrived in New York, those first few weeks on B, I gave a dime or a quarter to everyone who asked. But after I had lived there for a while, I started to say no. *A trembling guy in blue asking for a buck. Startled, I refused. Am learning to be harder-hearted, faster. Don't like it. But also feel defensive, poor. Can't give bucks away like that.*

By the time I left B, that hard-heartedness had become ingrained. I gave to musicians (when I liked their music), and I gave to women (or tried to). But for the rest I listened with only half an ear. I went on reading, looked the other way. *I'm sitting down*, I told myself. *I can't get at the pocket with my money in it.* Or, *This problem is too big for me. This is the responsibility of the city, the state, the federal government.*

Excuses, more excuses, as if *no* was an armour that I needed to survive. A high cost armour, it turned out, for everyone concerned.

Early this spring, I was sitting with my friend Elizabeth

in Union Square, idly glancing at the passers-by. An elderly woman stopped at the corner, and began rifling through the garbage for a slice of half-eaten pizza. I watched attentively. *I must put that in a poem*, I thought. It was only when Elizabeth suggested that we buy the woman lunch that I realized (really realized) that this was a real person. Action could be taken. Something could be done.

I glimpsed that same estrangement, that half-conscious brutality in an Asian photographer at the Second Avenue subway station. He had stopped to take a picture of a homeless man sprawled out along the steps, his head resting on a battered knapsack. *Click!* went the camera. And again, *click!* There was no human contact, no offer of money. The man had been symbol merely: the 'Lower East Side of Today', *take one, take two*.

The stories people tell about their survival in New York are often the anecdotal stories, my friend Bartlett's tale of waking up one morning to find a cockroach crawling up her nose, the dead rat I found under the kitchen sink, *heavy, fruity, alarmingly alert, almost dog-like in its decay*. It makes sense that this should be so. It is easier to talk about the cockroach and the rat than about homelessness or gentrification or the drug-scene, at least in any full and complex way. Admitting the tangle of feelings: fear and compassion and anger, selfishness, numbness, impatience, can be a frightening and painful thing to do. How much simpler to look the other way, to cross the street when someone asks for help, to hide our confusion even from ourselves.

When I moved back to New York for the second time, I had a job in Coney Island, working with Adult Literacy through the Brooklyn Public Library. I was editing two anthologies for Virago, and doing little pieces of my own work on the side. I was not alone and helpless. I had a lover (at least for some parts of that time), and an increasing circle of friends.

And yet, when I try to remember how things were — not for the Puerto Rican woman underneath me who yelled through the ceiling when her husband beat her up, not for the Indian waiters on the second floor living eight and ten to one apartment — but for me, myself, I, my immediate neighbours and closest friends, a frightened clenching starts under my ribs. I remember the anxiety and desperation, the talk of time and shrinks and real-estate, the nervy messages on answering-machines. I remember how it was to ride the subway two and a half hours a day, the rage that filled me as I finally got *out*, wanting to kick the innocent calves of the person two steps ahead of me, wanting to move fast and freely, not to be stopped short at the endless traffic-lights: *Walk/Don't Walk*.

The first years in New York had been, for all their terror, vivid and exhilarating. I lived them, I now see, as a kind of adventure-story. Even the 'good works' I did: attending block meetings, taking part in a march to defend Loisaida, working a little in a local soup-kitchen, had some self-consciousness to them, some strain of anthropological investigation. They satisfied my notion of the 'artist's apprenticeship'.

After my brother and my sister died, the idea of 'pursuing difficulty' lost almost all its interest for me. I was far more concerned with the quality of daily life. I wanted warmth and strength and friends and conversations. I wanted to build a world that would sustain me. It wasn't easy. No one I knew had any time to spare. There was in general no time to babysit, no time to help a friend move, no time to ask

— 118 —

someone over for a comfortable British cup of tea. What couldn't be solved professionally ('See an analyst, an accountant, a realtor') or on the telephone ('Leave a message when you hear the beep') was often left unsolved altogether. It was nobody's fault exactly. New York was just like that: too fast, too self-obsessed. The poor, the old, the needy, suffered most. 'We are throwaways, we are discarded', a woman in her seventies told me. 'No one has time for us'. And she was right. In a city where the demands were so enormous, where you had to schedule an evening at home to clean the house and do your ironing, there really wasn't very much left over.

In the old Algonquin language, Manhattan means 'the island of the hills'. Given the emotional and practical terrain, I have often felt it should be 'the island of the rocks' (or even 'on the rocks'). But as a new piece of graffiti informed me recently, 'GOD IS WEIRD'. However you define New York, the opposite of what you say is also true. The other side of drugs and homelessness and stress is strength and sanity and political activism. And these things do exist. The neighborhood itself, with its homesteading projects and community gardens, its legal advice centers and its labor unions, its churches and synagogues and theaters and schools, remains, despite everything, resilient and inventive.

Nina lives in Massachusetts now. She has finished her first novel, and is building herself a cabin in the woods. Gloria Anzaldua has moved to California. Turk left town, and nobody has heard from him since. But Deborah still lives on B, opposite the shooting-gallery-now-turned-condominium. She is married, and her glossy black hair has silver streaks in it, but she calls herself 'Doctor Comfort' and works as a clown in children's wards all over the city. Because I live around the corner (on Third Street between

A and B), we see each other often. We go to plays and movies together, talk on the phone, take walks in Central Park. If we ever leave New York, we say, we'll try to head for the same territory.

Poem of the Tree

CHRISTIAN MCEWEN

I am the tree
and the child climbing me
has put her small left hand with the freckle on the palm
on the lowest of my branches.
I can feel her stubborn pulse
beating in her wrist.

I am the tree
and the child climbing me
has swung her feet into the air
and set her shoes upon my trunk.
She has hoisted herself up
into the lowest of my branches.

I am the tree
and the child climbing me
is waiting for a moment with her face against my thigh.
And I am waiting too
just barely breathing.
I am standing with my arms around her waist.

I am the tree
and the child climbing me
is reaching for my shoulder.
She is feeling for the small bones of my neck.
Her hands are in my hair and we are swaying
both of us are tremulous and swaying.

Her stubborn heart is beating in my chest.

Earls Court

EDWIN MORGAN

I love a bristly kiss. What was it Brooke said,
the rough male kiss of blankets. Don't tell me.
Standing with Peter at the window,
his streaky jeans against the orange duvet,
his quizzical unshaved face as close as a map.
Outside, a frosty morning in Earls Court.
The milk-van purred along. Milkman,
milkman! He's seen it all before.
His Mexican moustache grins the bottles down.
He's off. The Glasgow plane's in Cromwell Road.
At 24,000 feet above Birmingham,
Manchester, and the sudden
startling flash of the Solway
I often thought of it,
wondering it hadn't faded
in the business of airports,
baggage strike, late take-off
— a moment of affection.

Tram-Ride, 1939 (F.M.)

EDWIN MORGAN

How cold it is to stand on the street corner
at nineteen, in the foggy Glasgow winter,
with pinched white face and hands in pockets, straining
to catch that single stocky gallus figure
who might be anyone but was one only;
prowling a few feet — not too far! — glanced at
idly by the patient Cosmo queue, growing
exposed, your watch burning, how long now, yes but,
what, half an hour, some eyes saying, Stood up, eh? —
until the step has to be taken, casually,
you have to stroll off, what's won by staying?
he won't appear (he had simply forgotten,
you didn't know that then), and on the top deck
of a southbound tram you stare into the window
as it reflects a mask about to shake with
ridiculous but uncontrollable tears, a choking
you gulp back instantly, no one has heard it,
shameful — shameful — to be dominated
by such emotions as the busy tramful
of half indifferent, half curious folk would
mock at if they knew, and would they sometime,
in half a century perhaps, accept that love is
what it is, that tears are what they are, that
Jack can shiver in the numbing close-mouth
of missing dates for Jill or Jake, and suffer?

Monopoly

JANE HARRIS

THESE YOUR wee milk bottles? says Campbell. This where the milk comes out?

Uh-huh.

Can I get the milk? says Campbell. Does it come out for me?

Uh-huh.

We're supposed to be playing Monopoly by the way. Least that's what we told Campbell's mum.

We're needing the big bed in your room so's we can spread the board out, alright Mrs Campbell? I said. Oh aye. It's always Monopoly we say we're playing. Sometimes we do play it, just for show right. Personally I hate the game.

Campbell puts her mouth to one of the pink lumps on my chest. I can feel her nipples, the fold of her breasts. See sometimes I hate my stupid stuntit efforts. Campbell sucks. I'm like that, out of breath; it's a dead weird feeling, pure exciting.

See if my mum knew.

Of course no milk comes out. I hope not anyhow. I've not had a baby yet anyway. Campbell says she can have weans soon if she wants to. I asked mum about that and she said that was right what Campbell said. If that's what she's wanting, my mum said.

Mum's not that keen on Campbell. See Campbell's mum and dad used to stay up the Drum and my mum thinks she's a bad inflenze.

Course, to have weans you need boys. Campbell's been pure sucking up to boys recently by the way. Last week we were hanging about up the road as usual waiting for the van and this Smitty comes stoating along with his mates. First of all right she just ignored them right, just normal. Then she keeps asking us if they're looking over. So I says naw. Because they weren't. Then she starts shouting at them like a pure headcase, slagging them. So I says shut it but she wouldn't shut it so right then pure brassneck, they come over and she was like that, ending herself. Like a big daft lassie.

That Smitty's nearly seventeen. Fancies his barra. Campbell was like that, talking to him right, just ignoring me. I could of been emdy.

She gives me a thorough examnation. When she's the doctor she always says: I'm going to give you a really thorough examnation, Miss Ferguson. Not like me. I get bored real quick with arms and legs and stuff. I'm like that, just examning the intresting bits. This is just one of the games we've got by the way. We've got all kinds. My favrite is 'captured'. That's when one of us is prisner right and the other one's the capturer. And the capturer gets to do whatever they want to the prisner. That's pure brilliant. Campbell likes it too. She likes being the capturer.

Sumdy's comin up the stair.

That's the ball up on the slates.

If we'd of went in Campbell's room we'd of been left in peace. In here the place'll be going like a ferr cozits her mum and dad's room. I told her that the smornin stupid cow.

I'm like that, pulling my t-shirt down and tucking masel in. Panickstations. Monopoly pieces all over the shop man, in the covers, spilt across the board. I'm staring at them, kidding on I'm deciding my next move. But inside I'm thinking, emdy that knew enthin about Monoply'd be onty us: the wee dug and the racer in the middle of the board right, and there's a coupla hotels in the jail by the way.

It's Campbell's dad.

He says it's the two of us he's after and in he comes.

Me and Campbell look up from concentrating on our game, the both of us pure astonisht that it could be us he's looking for. Mr Campbell says he's been out the back and it's come to his attention that his gnome's got no head left. Been knocked right aff, he says.

He settles down on the bed like he's preparing hissel for a long wait at the bus-stop. He pushes his eyebrows up at us. I look over to Campbell, right, wondering if it's OK to laugh. It's not. Campbell's frowning away good style like she's trying to imagine what in heaven's name could of happened to the poor gnome's head. Which is intresting since it was her that threw the brick at it.

Mr Campbell's waiting. He makes a face like he's got all the time in the world. He's no bothered about the Monopoly. Obviously not an affishonado. He's tall, Campbell's dad. Old-fashioned looking.

Puts brillcream in his herr.

He looks right like one of they dads in the reading books we got in Primary school, the dads that were always in the garage sorting the car with the boy. Not like my dad, he's modren. My dad makes cakes for my mum when she's out at work. And we've no got a car.

My dad says that's because of the ozone layer.

It was me Mr Campbell, I say. I broke it.

Oh, says Campbell's dad. Right. He looks down at his shoes. He bends over and starts rubbing away at his toecaps, trying to get more of a shine on them.

Jacquie was away round the front, I say. We were play-ing, a … a game. I banged intit. It was a accident. Campbell's staring at me as if I'm pure mental by the way.

But she'd get skelped see, if he knew it was her. I'll get nothing.

Oh, says Campbell's dad again. He straightens up. He's got a big riddy from bending over. Well, Elspeth, he says. Just you be more careful.

Yes Mr Campbell.

Anyway, he says. Time yous two were getting interested in boys, not playing boys' games out the back eh. He pats Campbell on the leg. Aye, Jacqueline? he says.

Yes dad, says Campbell. She'll not look at me. She knows this is dodgy territry.

Where do yous stay? she said to that Smitty last week.

You know fine where they stay, I said. They're Drum boys. And she's like that, kicking us. So they said they stayed up Kinfauns and then she says that's where she used to stay before her mum and dad flitted. And that Smitty says who's this? pointing in my direction and Campbell looks at me and you'd swear she didn't know the answer by the way. Ventually she says: Just one of the lassies from Stonedyke, she says. Just one of the lassies. Then Smitty says, Oh aye, a snob, and Campbell doesn't say nothing, just blows a stoater with her hubbabubba. I'm not chewing mines but.

I'm just standing there with my mouth open.

Bealing.

Not that she'd of noticed, she was already up the road with Smitty and that. See you later, she shouts back. Chomping away at her hubba, making it go crack, crack. I'm telling you that's cruelty to bubblegum by the way.

Just as well she was away up the road but or I'd of punched her lamps out.

So she's not looking at me the now, because she knows what she'll get later. She's lucky I'm still speaking to her. I told her how it was going to be, she could have me and nobody else. Not Smitty, not any boy. And if I so much as saw her looking sideways at emdy, that'd be it. Jotters. I'd not come round any more and she'd always have to be on her tod. See, she's not got any other friends right, there's nobdy ages with her round here and all the one's my age don't like her cos she's weird.

So I just reminded her about that and I tellt her how it'd be.

See our Jacqueline's wearing a bra now Elspeth, says Campbell's dad. He says that every time I'm here. Every time. He's taking the mick right because I've not got one. He pings the strap.

Leave dad, just leave, says Campbell. Her face is all went pink.

Soon be shaving her armpits, he says. Me and her mother'll not be able to get into the bathroom. She'll be in there, shaving anything that moves. He laughs. He thinks this is a great joke. Funny thing when he laughs Mr Campbell, there's not much noise. He just sort of wheezes a bit and rocks backn forwars.

Look dad, just forget it, says Campbell. Okay? She's near enough bubbling. She comes round my side of the bed and starts picking oose off the covers.

Are you wanting money for your gnome, Mr Campbell?

Aye hen, he says. A hundred quid. He lifts a hundred pound note out of the bank and folds it into his pocket. Then he starts laughing again. Hee haw pure bloody hilarious Mr Campbell. Just don't let it happen again, he says, in between gasping. Okay? He's more weirder than Campbell is.

Okay, I say. He winks at the both of us then off he goes wheezing. Me and Campbell wait till he's down the stair then we start picknup the pieces of the game and putting them back in the box.

He'll not be back now, I say.

Campbell's saying nothing. She keeps shuffling the Chance cards.

Haw deafie, I say. What if we do 'captured'? C'mon, you can be the capturer and we can be, Americins, Americin spies. She likes that, specially, when we're Americins. We can do the ones she like more often then she'll not be bothered with that Smitty character.

She's still not saying nothing but. Taken the hump.

Sometimes I really like her by the way, then other times I'm like that, can't be bothered. She thinks she's brilliant know what I mean, just cos she's got a new bra and a couple herrs on her fanny.

Liaison

JOHN MCRAE

Lying together unsleeping after,
knowing that best
would be for one to go.

Absence now of all that
drove before — no thrill
at touch, undesired.

And a long time to go till morning.

A Tone

JOHN McRAE

Every generation must accept the anger of the young;
No good believing they will love what you have done.

He talked and talked in platitudes, then came to bed.
I felt older making love, weighed down by what he said.

Hustling the Copthorne room 432, Thursday at ten;
A lot to be learned in the world of loving men.

Pomegranate Seeds

JANE CARNALL

Myth: A Story that exists in the act of being retold.

LET'S SEE, how does the family tree go? Out of Chaos came Earth and Sky, and they had a son called Time, and Time cut his father Sky to bits. (One of the bits fell into the sea and from the foam that spurted up where it fell rose Aphrodite, god of love. Just one of those things that will happen even in the best regulated mythologies, and I warn you at the start, this is not.) Earth told Time that one of his children would be greater than him and destroy him. So when Time had six children, he swallowed each of them as soon as they were born. Except the last one, because their mother made Time swallow a stone instead. Perhaps baby gods don't taste that different from granite, and in any case Time is a notoriously careless eater.

So the youngest godlet grew up, became great and powerful, and killed Time. He also forced Time to vomit up his five sisters and brothers and the stone, which being such a significant stone probably fell straight to Scotland and became the Stone of Destiny[1], which is not in Westminster Abbey, whatever the English may tell you.

Zeus the thunderer and Hera the power of heroes became

---

1   Actually it fell first to Palestine to be Jacob's pillow when he dreamed of ladders, and was then transported to Ireland, and *then* went to Scotland. I'm shortening a little for the sake of the story. It still isn't in Westminster Abbey.

rulers of heaven. Hestia, the stay-at-heaven one, became ruler of the hearth. Poseidon became ruler of the sea, also earthquakes, horses, and bulls. Hades became ruler of the underworld, the lands of the dead. (There were three: a kind of ghostly limbo where the hordes of unimportant uninfluential dead went; the hell where strikingly evil people were punished with classical simplicity — water that drains away when you try to drink it, rocks that can never be rolled to the top of the hill, chairs that glue you to the seat, that sort of thing; and the Elysian fields, where the heroically dead went, to be visited and interviewed by epic poets.)

And Demeter became ruler of the earth, of green growing things, of harvests and fertility. Demeter had a daughter; her name was Persephone, and being a god she was as beautiful as she was good, and as good as she was wise, and as wise as she was beautiful; and if you disagreed, since you're a mere mortal, she would probably have blasted you.

One day as Persephone was out playing with her girlfriends, Hades came up out of the earth in a chariot (gods can do anything) and grabbed her and took her back down again to his underworld. The girlfriends went running off to tell Demeter.

Unfortunately, the only god who could *make* Hades give up his niece was Zeus, and Zeus was uninclined to help. A man had his needs, and Hades was his brother, and after all Persephone would be Queen of the Underworld, and that wasn't so bad. Great opportunity for the girl. Probably having the time of her life. Natural for a mother to be worried, but after all every daughter has to leave home some time, doesn't she? And so on.

Demeter was divinely pissed. When gods are furious, strange things happen. In this case, as Zeus was speaking, the first autumn came on earth; and by the time he'd gotten to the part about Persephone probably having the time of her life, it was winter, also for the first time. I imagine that the remark about it being natural for a mother to be worried probably resulted in the first ever blizzard.

The only gods who sympathised were Hecate, ruler of the night, and Hermes, god of thieves, travellers, and messenger to the dead. Hecate's fury is the reason why the nights are longer in winter; she and Demeter went walking together, and where they went the world withered and darkened.

Hermes, the only other immortal who had free passage into and out of the underworld, went down to Hades to fetch Persephone back. But before he could reach her, Persephone had been tricked by Hades into eating six seeds of a pomegranate. Therefore, though Hades had to let her go, in six months she would have to come back, and stay half a year, and so on forever.

And every time Persephone goes back to the underworld, Demeter and Hecate grow angry again, and green things wither and the nights grow longer. Never eat rubyfruit with strange gods, and remember, all Greek gods are strange in hell.

A Sunday Walk

MARY MCCANN

IT'S A SUNDAY, like any other: Jenny, forty-one, broad and quiet, makes for the woods. Underfoot, there's black mud, spiky green and white garlic, yellow stars of celandine. Her feet tread carefully in her heavy boots. The traffic noise from the street disappears. Jenny feels more and more at ease, moving at a steady pace towards the nature centre, her rendezvous with Pat and Laura. She hums a little. Pleasant thoughts. I'm going to meet my lover. More awkward thoughts. Am I getting used to being a lesbian yet. I can say I love Pat, Pat's a woman. She kicks a piece of branch. But the word lesbian sounds coarse. I don't like it. It's not me. She sighs. Pat uses the word with pride. I'm a lesbian, she says, smiling, dismissing all the disasters and sadnesses of trying to relate to men. Pat can write the word on walls with her thickest black felt-tip. Lesbians ignite. Jenny can't imagine being that strong.

The path bends left. All but blocking it is a large straggling family in bright jerseys, with several dogs and a clutch of children. Jenny squeezes past. She looks at a woman her own age, smiling, made up, glossy in her expensive casual clothes. Where did I go wrong. Could that be me if I'd only obeyed the rules. Then smiles. I've never been able to obey the rules.

She walks on. Muddy dogs, labradors and retrievers, gallop past her. Fathers throw sticks in the water for children. Jenny comes out of the tunnel-like path and sees the old house that is the nature centre. No sign of Pat yet, must have missed a bus. Calm and happy, she pokes around, finding a fallen tree, helping a child to climb over it. Frosty reception from child's mother. I look freaky I suppose, short hair, boots and very old clothes. In the distance she sees another child running. She wears a pink anorak and koala rucksack. She's laughing and waving. It's Laura. They shout and wave, meet and hug. Behind her Jenny sees the familiar shape of Pat. She hugs her as well. No kissing, too public. But I'll take her arm, they can't stop me doing this.

Running ahead, Laura finds a steep path up the bank, a challenge to a nine-year-old. Up they go, Pat last, hanging on to branches, panting happily at the top. Here is another path. They wander along quietly, Laura bouncing and humming, Pat and Jenny walking close and smiling at each other. Dogs visit them. Magpies whirr in the trees. Ahead, a grey fluid column drifts up among the trunks. Laura, sharp eyed, sees it first.

'What's that?'

'A tree on fire? Surely not!' says Pat.

No one can understand it. Smoke is pouring from ten feet up the trunk of a beech tree ahead. It's the odd one out, all the other strong straight trees are unharmed, one tree only is smoking. Like the burning bush, a sign, thinks Jenny in confusion. They reach it and stand to stare.

'The poor tree,' says Pat.

'Oh come on!' Laura tugs her arm. 'It's just a fire, it was probably boys that started it!'

From ground up to six feet, half the base of the tree has vanished and there is a black charred cavern instead, with ash at its foot. Smoke spurts from cracks in the trunk further up. Jenny stares at the live wood, the surface of the trunk greenish grey. It has wrinkles in it like her own skin.

'How can it burn?' she says. 'It's green'.

She feels very sad. Tree, tree, don't burn, don't die. She looks up. It towers up and up, a giant like all the trees around. Its base looks dangerously frail now.

'Can't we do anything?' says Pat.

They stand in a line, stricken. People pass, pause, say nothing, walk on guiltily. The burn chatters uselessly a hundred feet below.

'No bucket,' says Jenny in frustration.

'Come on!' Laura again. 'I want to climb the hill.'

'We'll tell the nature centre,' decides Jenny.

Pat is upset.

'They won't be open till tomorrow, this is Sunday'.

'It's all we can do,' says Jenny.

They write a note on a scrap of yellow paper from Pat's pocket. After all her objections, Laura insists on signing her name, a squiggly scrawl.

They walk on in silence. Jenny thinks of the night a crowd of local boys came after them, up at the high flats where Pat and Laura live, and the fear and panic she felt. She wonders if Pat is thinking of it too. But she decides not to mention it. She puts her arm through Pat's arm and hugs it. She looks at the shape of Pat's head, and her short blonde hair, and thinks: I love her. Almost immediately Laura tries to squeeze in between them. Gradually Jenny forgets the sad tree as they walk on, mixing talk, laughter, exasperation and closeness: the usual mixture when all three are out together. A bickering restless stage sets in. It's hard not to blame Laura for everything, it's always hard not to blame the smallest and neediest, thinks Jenny, as Laura bumps into her for the fortieth time and tries clumsily to take her arm.

They ramble on to the crags, climb up, over and down, back to the burn. It's time to turn for home. Jenny gives Laura a hug to make up for the bickering. She looks at Pat. I always feel the same when we leave each other. It just seems silly to separate. I've got used to being with her. I keep wanting to turn to her and put my arm round her shoulders, and say look at that, or tell me about this, or have you heard. ... Pat and she embrace quickly. They don't say any of this, just look at each other. They arrange to meet later at the meeting tonight. Now Pat needs to get home and eat, and see Laura's babysitter and pick up the articles for the meeting and get out again. What a rushed life, thinks Jenny. She turns for home. Turns again and waves. Her hand on the yellow note in her pocket to remind her, she marches off along the low path by the burn, back to the nature centre. Puts the note in the letterbox at the house and says, 'There, I did it,' to an absent Pat.

Turning for home she pauses at the low brick building which houses the toilets, a quick pee is needed. There are no doors, she just walks in to the Ladies. Dead leaves on the floor, a damp dingy smell. One cubicle and a hand basin in a dim lit space. A big black scrawl on the walls. Felt-tip. Jenny realises it's Pat's work, she told her on a previous walk she was going to graffiti the toilets. LESBIANS ARE EVERYWHERE, it says, loud and clear, linked women's symbols below. Jenny looks at it, and at what is written above it and overlapping, in blue felt-tip. FUCK YOU YOU SLAG, it says.

Feeling nothing, Jenny turns and enters the cubicle. EVERY WOMAN CAN BE A LESBIAN, she reads as she sits down. Under it the same blue felt-tip has written: EVERY WOMAN CAN SUCK COCK. Jenny gets out of the toilet very slowly and washes her hands in the freezing water. There is a space where her stomach ought to be. She doesn't approve of graffiti, does she? No. Messy and destructive. But that isn't it. It's the words. Fuck. Slag. Cock. Jenny looks again. They hate lesbians, she thinks, almost with surprise, as if a well-known fact in a book has leapt out in physical form and hit her over the head. They hate me. She stands very still.

She thinks of mothers at the school gate looking oddly at her when she goes sometimes to meet Laura. She thinks of the gang of boys throwing punches at her and Pat, up against a wall, no escape, and how Laura ran on and screamed till some girls ran down and stopped the boys. She wonders if it was a girl or a boy, a man or a woman, who wrote in blue felt-tip. She stands for a while longer, then, trembling, feels in her pocket for her pen. It is a thin fragile fine-point felt-tip. Under EVERY WOMAN CAN SUCK COCK she writes: Not me — I'm a lesbian, in small spidery writing. Under FUCK YOU YOU SLAG she writes: No way. The space in her stomach is filling up with a feeling she starts to recognise. It is anger, fire, strength. She walks out of the toilet into the green space and the sun.

Breathtaking Ignorance

Val McDermid

EVERY CATERER's nightmare. The choking customer, collapsed on the floor gasping for breath. I'd already hurtled through from the kitchen as soon as I heard the coughing and spluttering, and I made it to his side just as he slumped to the floor like a Bonfire Night guy, legs splayed, head lolling, eyes popping.

The boardroom crowd were keeping their distance, remembering all the strictures they'd ever heard about giving people air. There was a nervous hush, the only sound the croaking gasps of the man on the floor. I knew exactly who he was. Brian Bayley, chief legal executive of Kaymen Merchant Bank. But that didn't stop me kneeling down beside him and dragging him into a sitting position so I could perform the Heimlich manoeuvre. That's one of the many fascinating things you learn at catering college. You force the air out of their lungs, which forces free whatever is blocking their windpipe. The downside is that somebody usually ends up covered in sick.

Bayley was bright scarlet now, his lips turning an ominous blue. I got my arms round him, smelling the sweat that mingled with his expensive cologne. I contracted my arms, forcing his ribs inward. Nothing happened. His gasping sounded more frantic, less effective.

'I'll call an ambulance, Meg', John Collings said desperately, moving towards the boardroom 'phone. He'd organised this lunch, and I could see that this was the last contract for a boardroom thrash that I'd be getting from him.

I tried the manoeuvre again. This time, Bayley slumped heavily against me. The heaving in his chest seemed to have stopped. 'Oh my God', I said, 'He's stopped breathing.'

A couple of the other guests moved forward and gingerly pulled Bayley's still body away from me. I freed my skirt from under him and crawled round him on my knees, saying, 'Quick, the kiss of life.' Out of the corner of my eye, I could see John slam the 'phone down. In the corner behind him, Tessa, the waitress who'd served Bayley, was weeping quietly.

John's chief accountant had taken on the unenviable task of mouth-to-mouth resuscitation. Somehow, I knew he was wasting his time. I leaned back on my heels, muttering, 'I don't understand it. I just don't understand it.'

The ambulance crew arrived within five minutes and clamped an oxygen mask over his face. They strapped Bayley to a stretcher and I followed them down the corridor and into the lift. David Bromley, Bayley's deputy, climbed into the ambulance alongside me, looking questioningly at me.

'It was my food he was eating,' I said defensively. 'I want to make sure he's all right.'

'Looks a bit late for that,' he said. He didn't sound full of regrets.

At the hospital, David and I found a quiet corner near the WRVS coffee stall. I stared glumly at the floor and said, 'He didn't look like he was going to pull through.'

'No.' David agreed with a note almost of relish in his voice.

'You don't sound too upset,' I hazarded.

'That obvious, is it?' he asked pleasantly. 'No, I'm not upset. The guy is a complete shit. He's a tyrant at the office, and at home too from what I can gather. He says jump, the only question you're allowed to ask is, how high. He goes through secretaries like other people go through printer ribbons.'

'Oh God,' I groaned. 'So if he recovers, he'll probably sue me for negligence.'

'I doubt if he'd have a case — his own greed was too much of a contributory factor. I saw him stuffing those chicken canapés like there was no tomorrow,' David consoled me.

Before we could say more, a weary-looking woman in a white coat approached. 'Are you the two people who came in the ambulance with ...' she checked her clipboard. 'Brian Bayley?' We nodded. 'Are you related to Mr Bayley?'

We shook our heads. 'I'm a colleague,' David said.

'And I catered the lunch where Mr Bayley had his choking fit,' I revealed.

The doctor nodded. 'Can you tell me what Mr Bayley had to eat?'

'Just some canapés. That's all we'd served by then,' I said defensively.

'And what exactly was in the canapés?'

'There were two sorts,' I explained. 'Chicken, or smoked salmon and lobster.'

'Brian was eating the chicken ones,' David added helpfully.

The doctor looked slightly puzzled. 'Are you sure?'

'Of course I'm sure. He never touched fish.' David added, 'He wouldn't even have it on the menu if we were hosting a function.'

'Look,' I said, 'What exactly is the problem here?'

The doctor sighed. 'Mr Bayley has died, apparently as the result of going into anaphylactic shock.' We must both have looked bewildered, for she went on to explain. 'A profound allergic reaction. Essentially, the pathways in his respiratory tract just closed up. He couldn't physically get air into his lungs, so he asphyxiated. I've never heard of it being brought on by chicken, though. The most common cause is an allergic reaction to a bee sting,' she added helpfully.

'I know he was allergic to shellfish,' David offered. 'That's why he had this thing about not serving fish.'

'Oh my God,' I wailed. 'The lobster!' They both stared at me. 'I ground up the lobster shells into powder and mixed them with mayonnaise for the fish canapés. The mayo for the chicken ones had grilled red peppers mixed into it. They both looked the same. Surely there couldn't have been a mix-up in the kitchen?' I covered my face with my hands as I realised what I'd done.

Of course, they both fussed over me and insisted it wasn't my fault. I pulled myself together after a few minutes, then the doctor asked David about Bayley's next-of-kin. 'His wife's called Alexandra,' he told her, and recited their home number.

How did I know it was their home number? Oh, didn't I mention that Alexandra and I have been lovers for just over a year now? And that Brian was adamant that if she left him, he'd make sure she left without a penny from him? And, more importantly, that she'd never see her children again?

I just hope the mix-up with the mayo won't hurt my reputation for gourmet boardroom food too much.

A Video of My Father

PETER DANIELS

At ease among statisticians, he settles into his chair
to trace back his subject for the archives.
His developing concepts arise, like The Advancing Wave
of a Spatial Birth Process. My nonsense-mind is
daydreaming probabilities, how I am where I am.

Telling of southward-moving mathematicals, 'We
Scots ...' he remarks; taking me aback, though he keeps on
a few Scots consonants. Always he is fondest of Leeds:
his first job, the Wool Research Board, drawing out
meanings from thousands of snapped-off ends of yarn.

London-Jewish baby, carried back north to where
Grandmother's herring boat came in. Families don't
add up. Look for some balancing factors: at the piano,
grasping the precision of Chopin; learning from a neighbour
the reconstruction of a watch, counterpoint of ratios.

At home, interpreting Grandmother's cabbage soup, her
Yiddish-Russian, her mental arithmetic. Bar-Mitzvah:
God's rules to measure the arbitrary lives, the walk
from synagogue to tenement door. Desire for the true
parameters, from the simple Standard Deviation, to

The Maximum of a Random Walk. But where I have walked
is not his Edinburgh: this window, years after his mother
nailed it up. From her time, I have one early memory: the lace,
the teacups, Arthur's Seat, railings at Portobello. No Scot,
no Jew, it's not mine: except the remainder, recurring.

Excesses of the Prior of Inchcolm
Deposed from office, 1224

PETER DANIELS

A monk is illuminating
aspects of the deadlier sins.
The Prior is much in his mind.
The blue snake twined
round the capital of Pride
follows his long smooth shape.
Something of his in the smirk
of the Scarlet Whore.

The Prior does not inspect the work.
He strides freely, he is not afraid
of the hellfires they resentfully
score down for him. Along this road
he will elevate self and soul: to see
his priority shining out beyond
the stony shape of the cloistered island.

Adventurer

Andrew Martin

Uncle Harry got a wet day for his funeral. Rain came down on the few attending, not many left in the family now anyway, and he filled up the last lair. So there he was with Alexander Thomas and his Beloved Helen. I had never known them, they were a generation further back and Harry was Mum's uncle really, not mine. Afterwards lunch at the Tweeddale, for his family and the few friends who had survived Harry from his teaching days. Celery soup and lamb sandwiches. It was a Monday.

Miss Hutton button-holed me as I conveyed sherry, a wiry-haired woman, in her eighties I suppose.

'And you must be Wilma's boy? Harry often spoke of you. He followed your career with interest, was very proud.'

Really? She probably thought I should have repaid that interest with the occasional visit. I'd come years ago, when Dad was alive, twice perhaps. All I could recall was a white-haired man with tufty eyebrows. And a red hanky. Or was that Uncle Brian?

'Harry of course being a traveller himself always took an interest in foreign parts. I borrowed that Indian book you wrote from the Library on special request. Harry said Kashmir was just the same when he was there.'

What was a traveller? During the War I suppose. And no, I didn't actually write that Indian book, I just accompanied the author. I'm in the colour photos. I look good in shorts.

'And of course when he was in New Guinea, he was quite a trail blazer, got mixed up in the gold rush, and Amy Johnson flying round the world, and that film actor with the moustache.'

What was the old duck on about? There was a respite as she tucked into her soup, now getting cold. Roll crumbs were lodging in her whiskers. I wondered what she had taught. English? The one who forced the class through Sir Walter Scott? Or a Viking expert? No, she was the Geography teacher. If I asked her now, she would tell me the world's longest rivers, in order.

'Sorry, Miss Hutton, Amy Johnson and who, did you say?'

'Yes, the Amy Johnson who was the flying ace. Your Uncle Harry met her in New Guinea and bought her a Martini. No, tell a lie, it wasn't Amy Johnson at all, it was Amelia something, the American one, and I'm not altogether sure it was a Martini either, come to think of it. But she disappeared anyway, flew off the map, and the film star was that wild one, the one who drank himself to death.'

'Well, Uncle Harry certainly had some tall tales to tell. I had no idea, was he fond of a wee drink?'

Miss Hutton fixed eyes on me which had terrorized several Lowland generations. Still very blue, matching the pebble brooch on her twin set. I might be a noted author in her eyes, but I wasn't above being reprimanded for impudence.

'Nothing of the kind. It was Robin Hood you know, Errol Flynn. The one with the big willie — and how are you keeping, Mrs Davenport? Haven't seen you over the door for weeks. How's your leg?'

Miss Hutton turned to her left and engaged a frail lady in maroon in conversation. I closed my dropped jaw on a lamb sandwich.

Harry laughed to himself, and being dead, it was to himself. Well, that's exactly what that smart-arsed great nephew deserved. Taking the mickey out of Olive Hutton. Good old Olive, always knew when a sharp word was in order. Who did this William think he was anyway? Ring in his ear, and a pony tail like some girl out of *Bunty*, and sleeping with some Cambridge pederast to boot. Harry wasn't sure how he knew that, but he felt that was the truth of the matter. Did Wilma know? She did look pained, but maybe that was grief. Poor Wilma, not wearing well, black doesn't suit her anymore.

Harry felt a little odd, which perhaps was justified, floating or whatever he was doing in the function room of the Tweeddale, and watching his relatives eat his funeral meats. Coffee was being served now, but he couldn't smell it.

Fancy Olive Hutton remembering that story about Amelia Earhart. And Errol Flynn. Harry had got tipsy one Saturday, and out had come the whole story, or rather part of it. But surely Flynn's anatomy hadn't come up. Poor Olive had been rather keen on Harry when he arrived, fresh from the colonies as English teacher. All bleached and tanned, with a tea-chest of shells and bowls. Sunday matinée in the Peebles Picture House with 'Captain Blood' had rather undone all that. But Olive had sat by him through the tears and cocoa, and had swallowed her disappointment in a war-time romance. Nice bloke too, RAF, dark-haired, pity he had to go down so soon.

But what about Flynn? His memory was clearer now. In all the years of compromise and cottages, Harry often wondered if he had just imagined it. Certainly there had been a man in New Guinea, a muscled Australian with an Irish dash, but was it actually *him*? Oh no, couldn't have been, he told himself. And then, caught unawares by BBC 2,

'The Sea Hawk' would bring it all back, trumpets blaring, full sails billowing.

What Harry remembered was heat. Heat and rain. And whisky. Two young men eyeing one another in a tin shack bar in the New Guinea highlands, the year, oh, 1930 or '31. Harry was the shy one, the freckly Scotsman up from the coast to check on some red tape, and getting over malaria. The other was this Irishman or Australian in jodhpurs and crisp cotton. So cool and clean in this climate, how did he manage it? And so talkative, so funny, and handsome. So unlike the red-faced, red-necked Australians Harry met on the plantations, whose main interests were liquor bottles and native breasts. Not that this Flynn seemed adverse to those things either from his chat. But now it seemed that Harry was his main interest, or was that the whisky going to his head.

The Club was quiet that night. Ma Fleming behind the bar, King George and Queen Mary above it, looking down on two Brylcreemed heads. The corned-beef curry was good for a change Harry thought, as he scraped the tin plate and watched Flynn's hairy forearms. That's what the Tropics did for you, it made you aware of body hair. Flynn was telling a story. It concerned pearls, savages, the ritual deflowering of maidens, and a narrow escape from death. Life was a bit less complicated in North Berwick, Harry commented, not really believing the tale, but prepared to trust in the stare and the impudent, inviting grin. Flynn laughed, then yawned, flashing gold fillings, stretching his physique. The Tropics made you aware of physique too.

Yip, a quiet night in Ma Fleming's. How much more whisky before the uptight little clerk lost his head and invited him back to his bunk. Not much, thought Flynn, Harry was meeting his gaze now. The kill wasn't far off.

In rain like that you would never hear a murder, far less

the sounds of a little tropical sodomy, as Flynn's uptight little clerk found love unexpectedly.

Of course Flynn hadn't stayed. Harry woke alone and shared his scrambled eggs only with nausea. Later he went out on patrol as planned and, returning to the Club a few days later, found it full of farting Queenslanders. Nor was the corned-beef curry so appealing, and this time it was only David Copperfield he took to bed.

A postcard came later, two in fact, and Harry tucked them away, but Flynn himself was not seen again. At least not in the flesh.

Meanwhile the damp funeral party was breaking up. Wilma was shaking hands and that trendy son of hers (in black from head to toe, but that was style not grief) was being charming to old ladies again. Harry supposed he was thinking of the Will. Yes, Wilma got it all. Pity there hadn't been a man, no real companion in all those years. It had just never happened, but once or twice perhaps, it had come close. There had been fleeting good friends — the Maths teacher at Lanark for instance, David something, red-haired, a charmer. But he was transferred to Thurso, and they had lost touch in the fifties. Years later they'd met on the Dundee train, and he was shepherding ginger-headed grandchildren.

And now I'm dead anyway, whatever that means, and Wilma and that son of hers will be pawing the flat and burning up my life in the back garden. Good God, that boy has it all, marches, badges, magazines. No criminal record like me. Delicate subject that, for a teacher of the young and innocent. But Harry was too weary to pursue that one, and already the Tweeddale was fading.

Mum and I attacked the flat, a dusty business. I burned the letters on another Monday, a wash day, and the neighbours complained.

'William, did you have to swear at them?'

I was busy. There were snaps of effete Egyptians and Kashmiris, letters from window dressers in Princes Street, postcards from Glasgow waiters with poor grammar. I started off reading them, memorized a few choice bits, but then got bored.

Miss Hutton came round to collect a couple of pictures and some books.

'Ah well,' she said, 'a lonely life, a lonely existence,' and pushed some smouldering sheets back into the blaze with her stick.

'Freddie'll be buried over there I should think' and gestured towards a plum tree in the corner, then catching my look she added, 'they were devoted you know. Such a handsome wee fellow.' She paused for effect. 'But then terriers often are.'

Mum came out to offer her some tea, ushering her away from the singed pile of personal effects, but Miss Hutton turned and waved her stick in the air in my direction, as if it were a rapier perhaps.

'No letters from Errol Flynn, I suppose? Now, wouldn't those be worth a packet?'

And off she went chuckling.

What was all that nonsense? An old queen's fantasy? I tipped the rest on the fire, florid signatures took light. Paul, Alastair, Lulu, Errol? Later I rang my lover in Cambridge, and told him of the windfall Mum was planning for me. We'd have new suits for a start, and maybe he'd actually write another book if we had a word processor to encourage him, and six months in Peru to inspire him. And we giggled over Harry and his lavender-scented letters, and congratulated ourselves on being so young and handsome and oh so clever.

It looked like a forest, an old-fashioned forest. All oak and ash and very green, not one of those Norwegian efforts that were everywhere nowadays. Birds were twittering, deer were running in the distance, and streams were tinkling close by. Harry wandered on, a little bewildered. His legs felt better though, and he seemed — what? Younger, straighter, happier, filled with well-being, even smelling rather nice. At peace. Of course he was bloody well at peace, he was dead. And if he was dead, then this green place must be ...

Suddenly he was slapped heavily on the back.

'This ain't fuckin' Heaven, Harry' cried a familiar voice, and he turned, bewildered, but strangely reassured.
'Welcome to Sherwood, sorry about the tights.'

Tourist

ELLEN GALFORD

'Edinburg?'

'Edinburgh.'

'Edinburrow?'

'EdinbURGH!'

'Edinbudda? Goddamit, Donny, I just can't get my tongue round the 'rgh'.

'Why don't we just call it "that neat little Scotch place with the castle?"'

Don cringes. 'You want people to think we're American tourists, or something?'

As if there could be any mistake. Here we are, talking that crucial half-decibel louder than anyone else on the train. Sporting creaseless leisurewear in ice-cream colours.

Don turns, for consolation, to his British Rail sandwich. Quickly retreats, spluttering.

'My god! What is this garbage?'

'Corned-beef and something. It was all they had left. They were closing down before Newcastle.'

He lifts the bread, peers and sniffs. 'That's not like any corned-beef I've ever seen before. I can't eat this stuff.'

Nancy wags her finger at him. 'Donald, I'm astonished. A sample of your very own ancestral ethnic cuisine, and you call it garbage. What would your poor old great-great grandma from Scotland say?'

He grins, stretches across the table and flaps the thing in

her face. 'You're right, Nan. I take it all back. Wanna bite? It's r-e-al g-o-od!'

Don likes Nancy. They get on fine. Maybe she should be the one married to him. But that would leave me paired up with Chip. He's a sweet guy, a lot quieter than Donald, but I just don't see it. The thought of us in bed together is downright silly. Not that there's much to say about me and Don in that department.

Still, I slip into a little daydream about the probable reaction, back in Maple Park, if the four of us came home from our vacation all rearranged and wife-swapped. I can just see the looks we'd get as we shopped for bathroom accessories at Shadyside Mall. Chip and I would lose our teaching jobs at the high school. (On second thought, they'd probably just fire me. The woman always pays.) Don, on the other hand, would sell more Toyotas than ever. The whole town would go trailing out to his showroom just to sneak a look. And, as Don always says, once you've got them in the door you're two-thirds of the way to a sale. He'd make a fortune, and Nancy could tell Wesley & Son Attorneys-at-Law where to shove their lousy secretarial job.

Meanwhile, poor old Chip and I would be struggling along on his measly art-teacher's salary, so I'd have to work on the checkout at the Triple-A Market. Where everyone would stare at me. In the end, the pair of us would be forced to leave town, and find a New Life in Wyoming or Arizona. But I couldn't do that. I couldn't stand to be so far away from Jo-Ann.

R-r-r-rip. There goes my reverie. Not to mention my resolution. I've been keeping myself on strict rations. I am only allowed to think about her five times in any one day. Now here I've gone and used up my quota, and it's only just early afternoon. Maybe I won't count that dream just before our travel-alarm went off. I'm not even going to dwell on that. And it wasn't my fault if that woman in the hotel lobby was wearing the exact same scarf I'd just bought for Jo-Ann in Liberty's. And then, riding to the railroad station, the taxicab turned a sharp corner and threw me right against Nancy (the boys were perched in those little jump seats). I couldn't help but think about how different Nancy felt from Jo-Ann — all tight and bony around the hip.

Anyway, once the train pulled out, I was fine until York. Then we passed the backs of some old houses on the outskirts of the town. I started imagining how different my life would be if I were a woman living in one of those houses. And, once I start going down that What-If road, it's always hard to stop. I wound up wondering how things would have been if I hadn't said yes to Don on my 21st birthday. Somewhere in these meanderings, Jo-Ann sneaked into the picture again.

I put her firmly off the train at the next stop, along with some old ladies, and that nice family sitting across the way, whose children had voices like clear little bells.

Unfortunately, Jo-Ann climbs back on board shortly after the North Sea comes into view (her eyes are exactly that shade of bluey-grey), and insists on sticking herself between me and the scenery until we pull into Waverley Station. Which is named, so Don informs us, after the works of the nation's greatest author, Sir Walter Scott. Don hasn't read any of his stuff yet, but he says he's going to.

Edinburgh's even more beautiful than the brochures. The taxi takes us up this big hill that winds up by the castle, with a view of the town all spread out below. It's romantic as hell. Jo-Ann would adore it. She went to Quebec once on vacation, and has never stopped talking about how old-world-picturesque it was.

Damn! That's me well and truly over the quota. Okay,

I'll only let myself think about her twice tomorrow. Serves me right.

The landlady at our Bed & Breakfast is as cute as a button, and everything is shiny-clean, even though the rooms are a little chilly. The house is lovely, really old-fashioned. Our room has a huge bay-window, with a dressing table in it, and a real marble fireplace. I feel just like a character in a Victorian novel.

'Get your walking shoes on, folks, and let's move it!' shouts Don, banging on Chip and Nancy's door. 'The afternoon is still young. Remember, every daylight hour we waste costs us nineteen dollars and thirty-five cents per person!'

The four of us have to watch the pennies on this trip, even though we've been saving up for ages. We're not exactly your filthy-rich gringos, although Don should do OK once the business is more established. This is the first vacation we've had outside of the US of A. Usually we just go up to Don's parents' cabin at Indian Lake, although we did fly to Florida for our honeymoon.

Our friends all thought we were crazy to go to Europe. Weren't we afraid of terrorist bombs and pickpockets and things? But we just quoted them the crime figures for our own county, which doesn't even have a big city in it to mess up the statistics. That shut them up all right. Anyway, I think it's time we widened our horizons, and Donald's been talking for years about seeing the place his ancestors came from. He's really only one-quarter Scottish, but he says it's the quarter that counts.

We march off to the Castle, high up on that enormous lump of rock. It takes me a minute to catch my breath, once we climb up there, so I just stand on the ramparts enjoying the view. Nancy, next to me, looks as if she's going to faint.

'I think I need the ladies' room.'

We find it.

She rushes into one of those little cubicles and throws up.

'Okay now?' I say, taking a sneaky look at myself in the mirror, while she splashes cold water on her face. 'I always thought you were the fit one — all that tennis and jogging ...'

'Damn it, Pamela', she giggles, 'you've had your head in the clouds since we landed at Gatwick. I've been dropping hints all week — I'm pregnant.'

I know just what to do. There's a script we girls follow on all these occasions. I squeal with delight, pull her to me for a sisterly hug, push her away again so that I can hold her at arms' length and give her the once over.

'Marvellous! Oh, Nan, I'm so excited! And you look fantastic! When did you find out? When is it due?'

We babble on, while repairing our lipstick, about obstetricians, morning sickness and the advisability of washable wallpaper for the nursery.

'You'd better watch out', she twinkles, wagging a finger. 'They say pregnancy's contagious. It'll be your turn next.'

'Please God, not yet.' My reply comes out a little crisper than I meant it to.

The door opens and an elderly lady walks in. American like ourselves — I'm beginning to realise that you can tell by the raincoats. The natives must think we get them issued to us along with our passports.

'Excuse me', she says, 'but there's a message from the two gentlemen waiting outside. They want to know if you've been kidnapped by the headless ghost of Mary Queen of Scots.'

Don leads us relentlessly onwards. After the castle, we fit in a tour of the city on the open-air top of a double-decker bus, a quick pizza near the place where they burned the witches (tomorrow, Don decrees, we're going to eat Scottish food and nothing else) and a visit to a genuine Victorian pub near our B&B. It's amazing, all stained glass, coloured tiles, carved mahogany, incredibly ornate. The cigarette smoke nearly kills us. Nancy looks pale but determined, and sticks with orange juice. Chip and Don make friends with an old guy in a flat cap and a hard to understand accent (made worse because he doesn't seem to have too many teeth), who introduces us to the wonderful world of malt whiskies.

'The wine of the country' Don intones, treating his new friend to yet another round of the legendary twelve year old Ben Whatsisname. Chip and I have fallen by the wayside, two or three Bens back, and are on Coca-Colas.

Back at the B&B our room is freezing. When we get into bed (the sheets feel like glaciers) I give him the news about Nancy.

'I heard. Chip told me when you two were in the bathroom at the Castle. Nice, isn't it?'

Then he comes out with the usual spiel. 'Give me another year to firm up the business, and we'll start our family. You really don't mind waiting, do you, babe?'

'Nope.'

'It doesn't mean we can't go through the motions', he murmurs, sliding towards me. Luckily the effects of too much twelve year-old Ben whatsit and incomparably authentic Glen Somethingorother hit him before he gets past first base.

I lie there in the dark and treat myself to a slow-motion replay of the time Jo-Ann and I went on a trek along that upstate nature trail, hunting specimens for my tenth grade biology classes. We were gone for hours; didn't come back with so much as a tadpole.

I wish I'd stop doing this to myself. I told her I'd miss her, but I never knew how much. I try to distract myself by repeating all the song lyrics I can remember. It doesn't help. They're all too sexy. When I think about her it aches, but it's also exciting. I wonder if I'm some kind of masochist.

The next morning we do a route march down the Royal Mile to Holyrood Palace to see the room where the famous murder took place. On the way back uphill (this place is all ups and downs) we make a few stops at craft shops and a tartan store. Don studies a chart with a list of Scottish surnames and finds his family tartan — his is only a little subdivision of some bigger clan, which disappoints him, but it's a really nice, bright-coloured pattern. He buys himself a tie, and wants to get me a kilt in the same material.

'Check out the price tags,' I whisper. 'We can't afford it.'

Nancy, overhearing, says why don't I just buy the material and get it made into a kilt at home. 'You could have that dressmaker pal of yours do it — you know, whatshername, the girl on your street whose husband ran out on her.'

'He didn't run out. He was thrown out.'

'I'm sure she wouldn't charge much, you being a friend and all,' coaxes Nancy. 'Everybody says she's really good.'

'She is. She made my outfit for Don's tenth high-school reunion. Copied it from a picture in *Vogue*.'

I plunge into the space between two racks of tweed jackets. My face has gone as red as Don's ancestral plaid, remembering.

('Get Jo-Ann to make you something really classy for the reunion,' said Don. 'I want to show you off.')

And she did. It looked fantastic. I never wore anything half so glamorous in my whole life. What a perfectionist. I had to go over to her place for about half a million fittings. That was fun, though. Lots of laughs and gossip. When it was finished, and I tried it on, she spent ages getting the folds and pleats to hang just right. Turning me round and round. Patting and smoothing.

Finally she was satisfied.

'You look good enough to eat,' she said.

Her voice sounded different. Serious, a little shaky. And she wasn't smiling.

Then I looked at her, looking at me, and something clicked. So I reached out and did some patting and smoothing of my own.

That was how the whole damn thing got started.

After lunch in a really quaint little tearoom, we take a walk through the New Town. It's all very dignified and handsome: I think it's a little dull myself, but Chip — always the art teacher — goes on and on about the elegant proportions. Suddenly the skies open. We expected Scotland to be damp and drizzly, but this is a real skin-soaking downpour. Luckily, we're right in front of a little bookstore, a perfect place to duck in out of the rain.

Don, Chip and Nancy stop just inside the door, to check out a rack of Edinburgh postcards. But I head deeper into the shop. This is the sort of little British bookshop I've always dreamed about. Back home, at the Mall, we only have one of those big chain bookstores, the kind that sells mainly murder mysteries and diet books.

It doesn't take me more than half a minute's browsing to realise there's something a little different about this establishment. There are shelves marked 'Gay Men's Health Issues'; 'Sexual Politics'; 'Lesbian Fiction'. I sneak a look over at Don and Co., but they're still busy with the postcards.

One book has a picture of two women holding hands on the cover. When I flip it open I see that it comes from an American publisher. I can't believe it. Where do they sell this stuff? You sure don't find it at the Mall. Then I spot something calling itself an International Lesbian Guide. With a huge section covering the USA. I am just about to look up our home state when Don gives me a low whistle.

'Hey Pammy!'

I slip it back on to the pile, in case he sees it, and pick up a vegetarian cookbook. I pretend I didn't hear.

'Pamela!'

I look up. I see Chip and Nancy scuttling out the door.

'Hurry up! We have to go now!' Don gives a nervous glance at the young man at the cash desk, who seems completely unconcerned. 'Come on, we'll be late for our appointment!'

What on earth is he talking about? We're on vacation. We don't have any appointment. Nobody knows us. Nobody's expecting us. I open my mouth to say so then realise my throat feels full of sand. I glance out of the window. The rain is still hammering down.

He looks really desperate so I follow him out into the downpour.

'What's up with you guys?' I ask. 'Don't tell me you just shoplifted a whole bunch of postcards?'

Chip stands there trying to flag down a taxi as if his life depended on it. One stops and we bundle in.

'Now what was all that about?' I demand.

'Something funny about that place,' Don chortles.

Nancy giggles.

'Something downright queer about it, Chip, wouldn't you say?'

They're all laughing so much they're practically wetting their pants.

'You probably didn't notice, Miss On-Another-Planet,' explains Don, 'but that wasn't an ordinary store. That was a pervert shop.'

'What?'

'For h-o-m-o-s-e-x-u-a-l-s.'

'Come on, how can you tell? You guys never got more than three feet inside the door.'

Nancy glances at the driver. He is safe behind his sliding window, can't hear a thing. 'There were pictures ... two women kissing.'

'You bet!' Don puts in. 'And a pair of muscly guys with no shirts on holding hands.'

'Tell her about the bulletin board,' says Nancy.

'Posters saying things like Gay Men's Hillwalking Group. Women-only disco. We couldn't believe our eyes.'

'Little hand written cards — what was that one? — Oh yeah. Lesbian Wants Room in Women-Only Flat ...'

'Lesbian Wants Room in State Psychiatric Hospital, you mean!,' laughs Nancy.

We have dinner in a restaurant that serves genuine Scottish food. Everybody there is either American or Japanese. We try haggis. Not bad, as long as you don't think what it's made of. Over something called Meg Dod's Flummery (good, but very fattening) we make our plans for the next day. We're due to pick up our rented car in the afternoon, and then it's off for a tour of the Highlands before we head back down to London. Donald has worked out the details with military precision — and God help Glencoe if it isn't full of moody Scotch mist when we get there.

Chip says why don't we split up for the morning, and all do our own things. He'd really like to look at the paintings in that Greek temple of an art gallery on Princes Street, which he fully appreciates is not anybody else's idea of a good time, and Nancy wants to poke around the department stores.

'That's fine with us,' says Don. 'The guidebook gives the

address of the Public Record Office, so Pam and I can spend the morning doing a bit of research on our family tree.'

'*Our* family tree? *Your* family tree, sunshine. Mine is a combination of Polish, Swedish and Cherokee. Anyway, I don't want to spend my last morning in this town sitting in a library. I think I'd rather wander around the streets some more and soak up the atmosphere.'

Poor old Donny. He looks a little surprised. But no way is he going to act like a Bad Sport in front of Chip and Nancy.

No prizes for guessing where I'm going. But for some reason, I start to chicken out when I get to the bookshop door. I can see through the window — there are people inside. Women. This makes me a little nervous, so I take myself off for a little walk around the block. I wonder if Jo-Ann would think I was a coward, or if she'd be just as scared as I am. Either way, if she were with me now, we'd probably be laughing our heads off. I am allowed to think about Jo-Ann as much as I want today, because I was such a good, co-operative wife last night, when Don found it necessary to prove to himself (and to me) that he hadn't caught queerness from breathing the air in that bookshop.

On my second circuit of the block, I give myself a little talking-to. Travel is supposed to be about broadening the mind, kid. And you are as sure as hell not going to get a chance to look at interesting books like these back home in Maple Park. Nobody you know is going to see you here. You're just another tourist. So make hay while the sun shines.

I take a deep breath and here goes. It's just like the time I learned to swim at Girl Scout Camp. Jumping into the pond is the scariest part.

This time, the person sitting at the cash-register is a

woman, with very short hair and the longest, dangliest earrings I've ever seen. She must be one of Them or she wouldn't work here.

I start with the bulletin board by the door, the one the gang found so outrageous. Loads of people looking for places to live, a few others offering. Notices about protest demonstrations, benefit concerts and poetry readings. Advertisements for astrologers, upholsterers, a course in aromatherapy and massage (Jo-Ann would be interested in that one). Someone is offering a lift to London, for the Lesbian and Gay Pride March. Don and I once saw some pictures from a March like that in San Francisco, on Cable News Network. You should have heard what he had to say about it.

I can't imagine Jo-Ann and me marching up and down and waving a banner. For a start, she'd be afraid to get her picture in the papers. Because then Gary would come roaring back with some kind of court order, declaring her an unfit mother, and she'd lose the kids.

Anyway, what would our banner say? I know for a fact that Jo-Ann doesn't like the L-word. I asked her once if that's what she thought we were, and she got very upset. She said that lots of perfectly normal married people liked to have a thing going on the side and ours just happened to be with each other.

I didn't have any answer to that, but I felt a little depressed and stayed away from her for almost a week.

I wish we didn't have to leave town today; I could use about ten hours in this bookshop. If somebody's going to the trouble of writing and printing all these books, then there must be thousands of women in the world who read them. So where the hell are they?

I pick up a paperback of Lesbian Erotic Poetry and read it practically from cover to cover. If Don saw me, he would go berserk. But he's not here now, thank goodness, so back I go to that International Lesbian Guidebook. I find the section on our state — there's not nearly as much as there is for California or New York, but it's still pretty surprising. I have the feeling that there must be this whole other America, with the same place names and zip codes as the one I live in, but occupying a whole other dimension in space and time.

I can't believe the stuff there is within an hour's drive of Maple Park — discussion groups, a couple of bars (one is in a rough neighbourhood that I wouldn't drive through without locking my car doors and rolling up the windows, but the other one is probably okay), a women's cafe, even a Telephone Help and Information Line. I wonder about copying down the number and calling them up when I get home. But I can't think of what I'd talk about.

I have an inspiration. What the hell — I'll just buy the damned book, after all. There's no way I could hide it from Don in our luggage, so I ask the girl at the counter if they mail things overseas. They do. I pay for the book, turn down the corner of the page with the listings for our state, and give them Jo-Ann's address. Then, as an afterthought, I add the book of sexy love poems as well. Even though it costs a fortune I have the package sent airmail. It could even get to Maple Park before I do.

I must be crazy. What a gamble. Jo-Ann might love it, or she might hit the roof. But if she doesn't like getting books with That Word on them I'll take them back and keep them for myself. She can still have the Liberty scarf.

I feel a little dizzy. I don't have to meet the others for a couple of hours yet, so why don't I take out my little tourist map and see what other places of interest there are in the neighbourhood? The Botanical Gardens aren't far away, and the girl in the bookshop tells me which bus to take. She has a very pleasant smile and no visible horns on her head.

The Gardens are beautiful. They look and smell wonderful. I think I like them better than anything else I've seen in Edinburgh. I climb a grass-covered hill, and find a bench with a terrific view of the whole city, and the mountains behind it. I look at all the roofs and chimney-pots, and the rows of windows too far away to see into. Somewhere in those houses are women talking to each other on the telephone, offering rooms for rent and driving lessons and aromatherapy. Arranging to meet at the women-only disco. Using the L-word, not giving a damn about what anybody thinks. Making love with each other.

And in one of those buildings, in some public archive, is Donny, digging for the roots of his family tree. Blissfully unaware that a certain branch of it has just developed a serious crack.

That part makes me feel really shaky. More of a nightmare than a daydream. But if that's the only door to the other dimension, then I guess I have to walk through it. Or forget the whole damn thing and play What-If until I'm eighty-five.

Maybe I'd better start working out some plans. With Jo-Ann or without her.

I wish it were time to go home.

Incomplete Metaphor — to Juliet

KRISTIN HANNA

I could call her a rose
and often do, inside, when
her velvet touch slips
that deeply in, and would
loose my pretension, dispel
my cultivated mystery.
Both would slip away, slide
forgotten to an untidy heap
around my ankles
(my intellect, unwilling
to be so disarmed, would first
eclipse her with a metaphor).

I call her a rose.
The name could begin to touch
the feel of her against my skin,
the way I drink in her scent;
I touch her and tremble
in serene awe as,
like a rose, she opens
and signals a new season.

But a rose is small, fragile;
a rose can be grasped, contained
by my hand, plucked
and understood.

The Contributors

STEVE ANTHONY was born in 1958 and educated at the Universities of Hull and Stirling, where he took an MPhil in Modern Poetry. His poems have appeared in various magazines, including *Orbis*, *Clanjamfrie* and *Encounter*. In 1990 he appeared in two anthologies: *Take any Train: A Book of Gay Men's Poetry* (Oscars Press) and *The Gregory Anthology 1987-1990* (Hutchinson), after his Award in 1987. He was also a winner in the Bloodaxe Poetry Competition, 1987 and the Scottish Open Poetry Competition, 1988. His first full collection, *Echoes from the Canyon*, is awaiting publication.

JANE CARNALL was born in Edinburgh twenty-five years ago and still lives there with her cat and her computer. She has also written for *Gay Scotland*, the old letters page of *The Scotsman*, and various amateur publications. At present studying for a degree in computing, but she still wants to be a writer when she grows up. 'Pomegranate Seeds' is part of a mythery series, continued on next rock.

BOB CANT was born in Dundee and educated in Forfar. He was a member of the Gay Left collective, a supporter of Positive Images in Haringey and co-editor of *Radical Records* (Routledge, 1988). He lives in Edinburgh and goes swimming every day. He is now trying to write fiction and is preparing an oral history of Scottish gay men and lesbians.

MAYA CHOWDHRY is a writer, film-maker and photographer who works across, through and over these art forms, covering a wide range of experiences, issues and concerns. Her poetry is published in *Putting in the Pickle where the Jam should be*, 1989. In 1991 she was awarded a Sheffield City Council Script Development Fund loan towards developing a sixty-minute TV drama, 'Broken Promises'. She directed 'Running Gay' for

Channel Four's 1991 'Out' series. Her radio play *Monsoon* was selected for the Young Playwrights Festival. 'I want to capture my impressions as a Black woman of the world around me and present them to others. Pick up a pen, a camera, use your eyes, your ears, find your voice.'

SUZANNE DANCE lives in Edinburgh. She is a radical feminist, with a strong interest in women's spirituality. She was the co-founder of WITCH, Women's Theatre Group. Suzanne works as an actor and a community worker.

PETER DANIELS edited *Take any Train: A Book of Gay Men's Poetry* for Oscars Press in 1990. He has recently prepared versions of medieval lyrics for R.S. Taylor's novel *Mortimer's Deep* (Balnain Books, 1992). His great-grandparents came to Leith from the Baltic in the late nineteenth century; born in 1954, he grew up in Birmingham and now lives in London, but maintains a toehold on a spare room in Fife.

TONI DAVIDSON was born in Ayr in 1965. He compiled and edited the first anthology of Scottish lesbian and gay writing *And Thus Will I Freely Sing* (Polygon, 1989). Currently living in Glasgow he has contributed stories to *Gay Scotland*, *Square Peg* and other magazines, reviews for *Rouge* and is organising the third lesbian and gay writing event, 'Outward Gaze' for Mayfest 1992. 'Travel — Excerpt from Sksuhno' is one of forty pieces he is presently working on.

FLORENCE HAMILTON works at Sheba Feminist Press in London, where she has lived since 1970. She is currently writing a book on British feminists and imperialism in India in the 1920s and 30s which will be published by Pluto Press, and hopes to move back to Scotland in the not too distant future.

KRISTIN HANNA is a writer (of fiction, primarily), singer / songwriter / guitarist and perennial student. She grew up in Los Angeles, California and moved to Scotland in 1989; she now lives in Edinburgh with her partner Juliet and is a member of St John's Episcopal Church, Princes Street. She wishes to thank Jennifer and Shari for their patience and encouragement — and Juliet for everything.

JANE HARRIS, usually Glasgow-based, is currently undertaking an MA in Creative Writing at the University of East Anglia.

Some of her other fiction concerns male homosexuality and transvestism, and can be seen in *The Day I Met the Queen Mother* and *Scream If You Want to Go Faster* (New Writing Scotland, 8 and 9, published by the Association for Scottish Literary Studies).

HUBERT KENNEDY has long been a student of the life and writings of the Scottish-German anarchist John Henry Mackay (1864-1933). He translated two of Mackay's man / boy novels (*The Hustler*, 1985 and *Fenny Skaller*, 1988) and is the author of *Anarchist der Liebe: John Henry Mackay als Sagitta* (1989) as well as several articles about Mackay in English and German. He now lives in San Francisco, where he is manuscript editor of the *Journal of Homosexuality*.

MARY MCCANN lives in a Scottish city keeking timidly out of the closet and wondering if it is safe to venture further. She had a story in *In and Out of Time* (Onlywomen Press, 1990) under a pen name, so this biographical note represents progress.

ALASTAIR S. MACMILLAN was born in Aberdeen in 1951; graduated Aberdeen University 1973; Youth and Community Course, Manchester Polytechnic, 1974; Community Worker in Northfield, Aberdeen, 1975; Co-founder / Co-ordinator of Guizer Theatre Company, Aberdeen 1976-81; Co-founder / Artistic Director of Krazy Kat Theatre Company 1st April 1982 and still flourishing. Currently Theatre Animateur for Essex County Council. Writing history: editor of some local Aberdeen anthologies, including *Machars '73*. He has had poems published in *Words (11-12)*, *Gay Scotland*, *Northern Light* (1980) and an anthology of Aberdeen poets *Setting Out* (Triangle Press, 1972).

VAL MCDERMID was born in Kirkcaldy, Fife in 1955. She achieved the questionable distinction of being the first Kirkcaldy High School pupil to graduate from Oxford; the descent continued and she spent the next fifteen years climbing the greasy pole of tabloid journalism in Glasgow and Manchester. She is now a full-time crime fiction writer (*Report for Murder*, *Common Murder*, *Final Edition* and *Dead Beat*) and lives on the edge of the West Pennine moors.

CHRISTIAN MCEWEN was born in London in 1956, and grew up in the Borders of Scotland. She has been living in the States for most of the past ten years, first as a student, and later as a teacher, editor, gardener and carpenter. She currently works as a writer with the Teachers and Writers Collaborative in New York City. *Out the Other Side: Contemporary Lesbian Writing*, which she co-edited with Sue O'Sullivan, won a Lambda Literary Award in 1990.

JOHN MCRAE was born in Perth and brought up in various parts of Scotland, finally Ibrox and Uddingston. He has lived in Italy since 1974, and currently travels the world lecturing and performing, while holding down jobs in the University of Naples and as Director of International House, Naples. Editor and author of many academic books, his poems are included in various anthologies, and in the volume *So Long Desired* with James Kirkup. He has read his poems in many places, from the Poetry Society in London to a Commonwealth Literature Conference in Dhaka, Bangladesh.

ANDREW MARTIN was born in Moffat in 1958. After some years in England and the South Pacific, he is now back in Scotland and lives in Edinburgh.

SUSAN MATASOVSKA was born in London in 1951. She has been a musician from the age of five and a writer from the age of eighteen, when she wrote a poem because someone else in her class had written one and she reckoned she could do as well. She spent eight years being a musicologist, followed that by playing the violin professionally in Vienna and Johannesburg and came back to the UK in 1985, where she now teaches the violin for her sins. She lives with her daughter Ursula and a black bitch called Susy. She has been published as a musicologist and editor, music critic and a poet (in both English and German). A member of the Edinburgh-based women's writing group Pomegranate, her poetry has appeared in magazines as diverse as *AMF*, *Graffiti* and *Log* (Vienna) and she has contributed to the Stramullion anthology of women's poetry, *Fresh Oceans*.

EDWIN MORGAN was born in Glasgow in 1920. His *Collected Poems* appeared in 1990, together with a book of interviews, *Nothing Not Giving Messages* and *Crossing the Border*, a collection of essays on Scottish literature. His latest poems are in *Hold Hands Among the Atoms* (Mariscat Press, 1991).

Contributors

DAVID PARLANE was born in Glasgow in 1959 and is employed there as a teacher of French.

ANDREW STAFFORD was born in Dundee and is twenty-six years old. He is an electronics engineer and has 'served time' with the Royal Air Force. He has travelled extensively throughout the world and is an avid supporter of the Arts. He now lives in the Stirling area but works mainly abroad.

MAUD SULTER was born in Glasgow in 1960. Currently MoMart Artist in Residence at the Tate Gallery, Liverpool 1990 / 91. Books of poetry include *As a Blackwoman* (1985) and *Zabat: Poetics of a Family Tree* (1990). *Necropolis*, her first novel, was published by Urban Fox Press in the autumn of 1991.

ALAN DAVID TAYLOR has always written about the experiences that shaped and reflected his developing sexual identity, but it took him until his early thirties before he placed that experience and that expression at the centre of his writing. There is now an urgency and an importance to that writing, because it finally places the author at the heart of attempting to write well. 'A kiss that lingered' is one of the products of that integration, and is concerned with the importance of the most intimate of connections which, pure and simple as it is, becomes the entry point to the most lingering of dramas.

MICHAEL VERINO writes: 'A note on Hart Crane. A gay American poet, Harold Hart Crane was born in Ohio in 1899, the son of a candy manufacturer. During his short lifetime he published only two books, *White Buildings* (1926) and *The Bridge* (1930). In 1932 he committed suicide by jumping from a steamship into the sea northwest of Havana on a voyage home from Mexico. Many of his finest poems were inspired by his love of men, especially sailors.'

RONNIE WALSH is twenty-six and now lives in Edinburgh. He studied Classics at Glasgow University and so is now 'between jobs'. He delights in Zenful things like cats, kaleidoscopes and the music of Enigma.

KAY WEST works in the leisure industry, is interested in the issues around women and sport and has had an article published in a sports magazine. '"The Single Bed Years" is my first piece of fiction to be published and is specially dedicated to L.A.W.

When not working or writing I spend my time socialising in Aberdeen, Glasgow and Edinburgh!'

CHRISTOPHER WHYTE was born in Glasgow in 1952 and was educated at St Aloysius College, then at Cambridge and Perugia. He returned to Scotland in 1985 after eleven years in Italy and now teaches Scottish literature at Glasgow University. His first collection of poems, *Virsgeul*, was published in 1991 by Gairm.

KENNEDY WILSON was born in 1957 in Johannesburg of Scottish parents. The family returned to Glasgow in 1960. In 1978 he went to college in Aberdeen after which he settled in Edinburgh. After working in advertising and PR he became a freelance critic and feature writer in 1988. A former arts editor on *Gay Scotland* he is currently an associate editor of *Portfolio*, the magazine of independent photography in Scotland.

JOANNE WINNING was born in London of Scottish parents in 1968. She studied English at Edinburgh University and is currently carrying out PhD research into female modernists. Having come out in Edinburgh, the city will always be intimately connected with her lesbian identity.

GRAEME WOOLASTON grew up in Stirling, lived in the South of England for many years, and now works in Glasgow as an arts administrator. He is a regular contributor of features and reviews to *Gay Times*, loves pubs, Mozart and leather (not necessarily in that order).

Other books from Polygon

And Thus Will I Freely Sing

Edited by Toni Davidson

£5.95 paperback

An anthology of Scottish gay and lesbian writing. This collection of poems, stories, autobiography and interviews was the first of its kind. With an introduction by Edwin Morgan.

'Toni Davidson is to be congratulated on bringing together this first collection of Scottish gay and lesbian writing, and as a first collection it rightly covers a wide range of material - documentary, prose, fiction, and verse. The tone of the contributions varies from the highly assured to the tentative, but a recurring note of painful and sometimes very moving honesty shows just how important such a collection must be as a first move towards greater openness. Particularly at a time when Section 28 allows an as yet undefined but potentially very oppressive threat to hang over the presentation of gay material, it seems all the more necessary to defend the freedom to publish work based on this inescapable part of human experience.'

Edwin Morgan, from his introduction.

'It is the honesty and conviction of *ATWIFS* that gives the work its strength.'

Cencrastus

'Wonderful stuff!'

Gay Times

'An attempt to break new ground.'

Square Peg

Towards the End

Joseph Mills

£7.95 paperback

Towards the End is the story of Paul Robinson from his final days at school in a small Lanarkshire town, through his first job in a bank, to his attempts to find companionship in the Glaswegian gay scene.

The novel centres on his first relationship with Alex, an older colleague from the bank who seems able to play the double game with ease. Their affair is under continual strain, their bond is essentially physical. Love remains an unspoken word between them, while Alex has a wife to consider, and Paul has yet to tell his parents...

This novel provides an angular perspective on class and clique protocol, while illuminating a previously hidden aspect of the city of Glasgow.

'... engaging.'

Times Literary Supplement

'*Towards the End* is a homely and honest novel with a simple plot of a first relationship which many will recognise.'

Rouge

All Polygon books are available from your nearest bookshop, or
can be ordered direct from the publisher.
Specify the titles you require and fill in the form below.

Send to: Polygon, 22 George Square, Edinburgh, EH8 9LF
               Tel: 031 650 4689, Fax: 031 662 0053

I enclose a cheque made payable to Polygon for £............

Please debit my VISA/Mastercard

(p&p is included for UK orders, please add £1.80 per book for overseas
orders.)

NAME..

ADDRESS*...

....

....

POSTCODE...

CARD EXPIRY DATE...
*Supply both delivery address & cardholder's address if different.

☐   Tick here for a copy of our recent catalogue.